Birds as Pets

Other books by Paul Villiard

Reptiles as Pets

Exotic Fish as Pets

Wild Mammals as Pets

Insects as Pets

Through the Seasons with a Camera

Moths and How to Rear Them

A First Book of Jewelrymaking

A First Book of Ceramics

A First Book of Leatherworking

A First Book of Enameling

A Manual of Veneering

Handyman's Plumbing and Heating Guide

Growing Pains

The Practical Candymaking Cookbook

Shells / Homes in the Sea

Collecting Stamps

Birds As Pets

With 75 photographs by the author

Paul Villiard

Doubleday & Company, Inc.
Garden City, New York

Library of Congress Cataloging in Publication Data

Villiard, Paul.
     Birds as pets.

     SUMMARY: Considers the care, food, and housing needed for a
variety of birds kept as pets.
     1. Cage-birds—Juvenile literature. [1. Birds.
2. Pets] I. Title.
SF461.V53   636.6′86
ISBN 0-385-03226-9 Trade
ISBN 0-385-04337-6 Prebound
Library of Congress Catalog Card Number 73–20722

For Vicky Frey
and
William Holohan
who were of great help

Acknowledgments

My thanks are extended to the Lustar Products Company of Springfield, New Jersey, for supplying me with the bird baths and feeders used in this book.

Thanks are also tendered to the Hendryx and Prevue Cage Company of Chicago, Illinois, for generously providing the assortment of beautiful hanging and floor cages illustrated in this book.

And to the Georgia-Tennessee Mining and Chemical Company in Atlanta, Georgia, which manufactures that useful material called Cat Comfort. This litter is great for the floors of aviaries and large cages, as well as for the purpose for which it is intended.

Contents

Birds as Pets

Preface

Throughout the world, the keeping of animal pets has reached proportions so great that it would be impossible to estimate the number of persons involved. In the United States alone, the pet business takes in many hundreds of millions of dollars each year. In 1971 alone, the amount of money spent on veterinarian and health service for pets in the United States ran nearly one half billion dollars. This does not include the initial cost of the animal or bird, nor the cages, equipment, food, and other necessities that go with the keeping of a pet.

At least since the time of the Egyptian Pharaohs, men have kept animals in captivity, either for sport and fighting, or as pets. Birds were also very popular, especially in China and the other oriental countries. In the early days, Canaries were unknown, since they originally came from the Canary Islands and the Azores. They were not discovered until around the 1300s by Portuguese explorers.

Most of the birds kept in captivity were Parrots or parrotlike species, and it was early discovered that these birds were capable of mimicking human speech. Training them, however, was done differently than it is today. The birds were hit over the head with an iron rod to make them speak! How many succumbed to fractured skulls before they could learn a word or two is not known, but certainly those captive creatures must have led miserable existences for the most part.

Birds were generally available only to royal families or to the very wealthy, since the only specimens finding their way to civilized shores were brought in by sailors returning from a lengthy voyage to the exotic places where the birds lived. A systemized method of breeding was unknown in the beginning.

Later, much interbreeding and crossbreeding of birds, were done in foreign countries. Now we have cage birds that in no way resemble the original stock. Fancy feathers, colors, body shape, and song have been bred into the various species.

Until recently, most birds sold in this country were imported from other lands. The raising of birds in captivity has reached the point where most of the specimens sold in pet stores are bred rather than caught in the wild. I am speaking mainly of the small birds like Canaries and Budgerigars, although the latter are still wild-caught in great numbers.

Birds—some birds—live a long time if they are cared for properly. Fifteen years is not at all unusual for a canary, for example. But they must be cared for. They cannot be neglected, so before you undertake to keep a pet bird, you should be made aware of the fact that keeping a bird does not mean buying it, popping it into a cage, and then paying some attention to it *if* you happen to think about it. Birds require daily care, and unless you are prepared to give them this, it would be better if you did not get one, since it would only lead a short and miserable life.

Birds are not really alarming carriers of disease, but they *are* responsible for two. *Psittacosis,* or "parrot fever," has been known for some time. A few years ago an epidemic was forecast in this country. Importation quarantine and subsequent health measures enforced by the government soon checked the advance of the disease to the point where it is no longer a threat to man to keep the hook-bills of the parrot family.

Now, however, comes along another ailment called *Reniket,* or Exotic Newcastle Disease. This is a virus which, being carried by wild birds, attacks domestic fowl, chickens, ducks, and the like, and is almost invariably fatal.

In order to protect our fowl farming, a law has been passed forbidding the importation of birds into the United States from all other countries. As a consequence, only birds bred in the United States are now available to persons wishing to buy them. For this reason, considerable attention will be paid to breeding in this book, since some readers may wish to try their hand at this very interesting and profitable hobby. Good luck.

Paul Villiard
Saugerties, New York

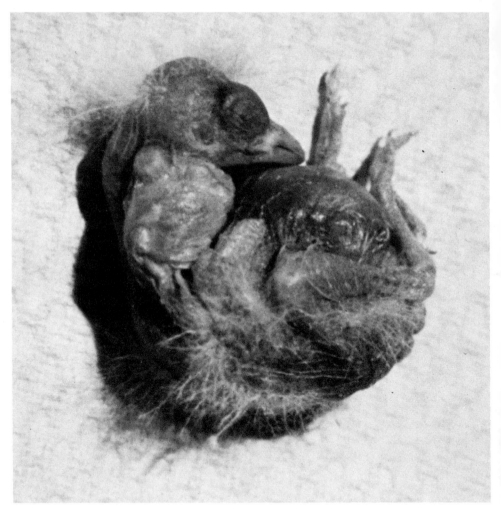

A Canary chick just one hour old.

A Little About Birds 1

Birds come in two kinds—*Altricial* and *Precocial*. Precocial comes from the same stem as the word precocious, meaning developed earlier than usual. And that is just what precocial birds are—developed. They are hatched almost completely feathered out and within minutes, or at most an hour or so, are able to run about and feed themselves, and they are not dependent upon their mothers for anything other than possibly warmth at night.

Altricial birds are hatched naked and helpless, with their eyes closed and their mouths open yelling for food. They are completely dependent upon their mothers for everything. The mother has to feed them. She has to keep them clean. Even when they finally feather out to the point where they can begin to fly, the mother must teach them to do this!

You were an altricial baby. When humans are born, they are naked and helpless. While their eyes may be open, they cannot see anything out of them. They must be fed, clothed, cleaned, and pampered. Deer, elephants, and most other animals are more precocial, since, wobbly at first, they learn within a matter of hours to stand alone, then run about following their mothers. They nurse for a time but eat other food as well.

Birds are, we believe, descended from the reptiles. This is not to say that birds replaced the reptiles, but they were an offshoot of reptile development. Certain characteristics indicate this. Birds, however, are unique in one thing—they have feathers, something no other living creature has.

Birds are believed to have started their development from reptile stock somewhere around 150 million years ago. Mammals had already evolved, so this makes birds the youngest group of animals.

There are about 8,600 species of birds now living, and scientists think there may be a hundred or more species yet to be discovered. Birds live in every climate and under every condition. From the frozen wasteland of the antarctic to the searing desert, birds, well adapted to their environment, are to be found. The foods birds eat are as varied as the birds themselves. Birds are fish eaters, vegetarians, carrion feeders, reptile eaters, insect eaters. Some eat only fruits, others only seeds. And there are some who combine several different things in their diets.

Birds are divided into 27 different orders. These are further divided into 155 families, each family containing from one to thousands of species. While several orders will be discussed in this book, we are mainly interested in just two—*Psittaciformes* and *Passeriformes*. To the former order belong the hook-billed birds like Parrots, Budgerigars, Parakeets, Lovebirds, Macaws, and several others. To the passeriformes belong the perching birds such as Canaries, Finches, Larks, Thrushes, and many, many other species. This huge order contains 55 families and over 5,000 species. Actually, Canaries are a kind of Finch, but more of this classification in the proper chapters.

The passerine birds are the most highly evolved of all birds and are the most recent development in the bird world. Passerines first appeared about 50 or 60 million years ago. Other orders go back 120 million years or even farther. Perhaps the most intelligent of the passerines are the Jays and Crows, including the Starlings. However, some of the Finches are also very intelligent. One Finch—Darwin's Finch of the Galápagos Islands—even uses a tool in order to capture its prey, succulent grubs in holes in trees. This Finch holds a long, sharp thorn in its bill, using it to probe for the grubs, then, when one is discovered, pierces it and hauls it out of its hole on the end of the thorn.

Some of the passerines are marvelous architects as well, building most complicated nests as a deterrent to predation. The Weaverbird is one of these and the nests are hung on the outer ends of branches. Whole colonies of birds build their nests in the same tree.

The construction of the body of a bird is rather wonderful. Everything is designed for lightness and for strength. The feathers are particularly interesting, having great structural strength as well as being practically weightless. The stiff quill is rigid for support at the base, tapering to a flexible tip at the outer end. From the quill, alternate barbs extend from each side. These barbs, in turn, are equipped with a series of hooks on their outer sides and filaments along the inner sides.

When the feather is preened into sleek smoothness, all the hooks are caught over the filaments, making a web, or flight surface, with which the bird can push against the air. Feathers can become disheveled either by getting caught in branches, in fighting with another bird, or by being caught by man. The bird is usually able to preen the feather back to its normal sleekness with its bill, using oil from a gland near the tail. This oil is also important in making the outer feathers waterproof in order to shed rain when the bird is caught without adequate shelter.

The contour feathers are the ones that make the outer shape of the bird, form the wings, and support it in flight. Under these are downy feathers called *Filoplumes*. Filoplumes are hairlike, and you may have seen them many times if you cook freshly killed chickens in your family. The "hairs" that must be singed from the chicken, prior to cooking, are filoplumes.

Many birds also have actual down feathers on their bodies. The down feathers are for insulation. Perhaps you have observed birds in cold weather, sitting on a branch, huddled together, their feathers all puffed up until the bird resembles a ball. This is because the down feathers are held erect to supply thicker insulation in order to combat the cold. It is like putting on an overcoat, since, by the erection of the down, the bird places a much thicker layer of feathers between its body and the elements.

Because feathers are subject to damage, they must be replaced. Once a year the bird is able to change its coat of feathers completely by the process known as molting. Some birds undergo an additional partial molt, but all birds molt completely once a year. As a rule they do not lose all their feathers at the same time. This would tend to eliminate the bird, since it would neither be able to fly nor to forage for food, to say nothing of the inability to escape its predators.

In most birds the molt is a symmetrical affair. A flight feather from one wing falls off, and its opposite number on the other wing follows at the same time. This leaves the bird with a hole in its flight feathers, but still able to fly and maneuver sufficiently well to survive. When these feathers have been renewed by replacement growth, another pair falls off. The growth of replacement feathers is rather rapid, and in a comparatively short time the molting process is completed, six weeks being the average.

Birds like this Cockatoo—and most other birds—have their eyes set at the sides of their heads. They can see frontward and backward.

Sometimes an artificial molt may attack birds, especially those kept in cages in the house. Too warm a location is not healthy for them. Birds can tolerate more coolness than you may think—it is drafts that quickly kill them. Even Canaries have been known to be bred and raised in outdoor temperatures through the winters, but they were protected completely from drafts and windy gusts.

The bones of a bird are another marvel of engineering. Since the creature must maneuver in the air, sometimes attaining great forward speed, its bone structure must be both light and strong. The skeleton of a small bird is practically weightless. The bones are hollow and the walls are thin. The backbone is fused for rigid strength instead of being flexible as your backbone is. The rib cage is fused together as two broad plates, and there is a keel on the breastbone to provide anchorage for the relatively enormous flight muscles. These may equal 25 per cent of the total weight of the bird, or even more in some species.

Compared to the birds, man is very nearly blind. Some birds, especially the birds of prey, have vision eight times keener than man's. Because the eyes of birds are set at the sides of their heads instead of on an equal plane in front—Owls being an exception—they have far better vision than does man. Birds have no trouble seeing behind them as well as to the sides and straight ahead. As a matter of fact, their monocular side vision usually overlaps both to the front and to the rear into binocular vision such as we have. At the worst, there is only a narrow band of blindness to the rear for most birds.

A Woodcock, with its eyes set higher on the head, and farther back than most birds, has binocular vision both to the front and to the rear. In this way it can watch for predators and attacks from behind while it is probing for worms with its long bill buried in the ground.

An Owl's eyes are very nearly immobile in its head, not revolving as are the eyeballs of a man. But it has the ability to turn its head in a complete half circle, to look straight to the rear or any angle in between. When an Owl sights in on its prey, it performs a curious sideways bobbing motion, to fix the range of the victim for the pounce.

The bills, or beaks, of birds are nearly as varied as the birds themselves. They are ideally suited to the needs of that particular species. Raptors—Hawks, Owls, Eagles, etc.—have hooked bills designed for tearing chunks from a carcass and for ripping off the hides of their animal prey. The large, strong, hooked bills of scavengers such as Vultures and Condors are just what are needed for ripping up carrion and rotting meat. The short, sharp bills of small perching birds cannot be bettered as seed-cracking devices.

Perhaps the most marvelous parts of perching birds are the feet. True, this part of the animal is not very pretty to look at. The legs and feet of most birds are covered with scales, pointing to their reptilian ancestry. They have long curving claws

Birds like this pet Great Horned Owl, playing with the author, can see only in front of them because their eyes are set very much like a human being's eyes.

which, in the case of birds kept in cages, must be periodically clipped. The wonderful part of a perching bird's foot is the musculature.

Perching birds perch on twigs and branches. They perform most of their life processes in this position, including sleep. Normally an animal relaxes when it sleeps, but if you ever tried to perch on a branch smaller than your feet, then tried to fall asleep, you would shortly find yourself flat on the ground beneath the tree. Not so perching birds. Their leg muscles are connected with those of the toes in such a manner that when the bird alights on a branch and squats slightly, bending its legs, the muscles pull the toes into a fist, clamping the branch tightly. As the bird relaxes, it squats lower and lower, placing more and more tightening effect on its toe muscles until not even a hard wind could blow it off the branch. In this way it is able to sleep safely and soundly, with no fear of falling off its perch.

Many of the small birds will breed in cages, and much work has been done by man to develop new strains, new colors, and improve the songs of such birds as Canaries and Finches. Several kinds of Canaries we see often in the pet stores are completely domestic breeds developed from the wild stock and unknown in nature. The wild Canaries only slightly resemble the birds we know. They are darker, mottled, greenish, and brownish. Their song, while sweet and clear, in no way is as beautiful as the song of a bred Roller or Chopper Canary.

Some of the other Finches will also breed in cages, and these are very popular cage pets. Budgerigars, Cockatiels, Parakeets, and Parrots can be bred—some easily, some with difficulty. Mynah birds have been known to breed in captivity, but only very rarely and not with much success. All Mynah birds in the country are imported, and now, with the new law that forbids bird importation in effect, it is doubtful if any more will be available. A fortune is waiting for the person who discovers how to breed them. One of the difficulties of breeding Mynahs is telling the sexes apart. Both the males and females look alike, and there is no sure and infallible way to distinguish them.

Some of the cage birds live for a long time. Canaries have been known to live for twenty-four years and longer. Parrots are the patriarchs of the cage birds, living for fifty years and sometimes much longer. This is a bird that you can get when you are very young, and grow up with. Peacocks can live over one hundred years.

Naturally, each species of bird requires some special kind of care and treatment, but all birds need much the same method of care for their health and welfare. Common sense is probably the most important ingredient for the successful keeping of bird pets. Unfortunately, this is not an item you can purchase in the pet shop where you go to buy your bird. You will have to work out common-sense methods for yourself, with the help of books on the subject. We will try to tell you here some of the ways to make the chore of birdkeeping less troublesome.

Because keeping a bird *is* trouble. It is a responsibility that you must be prepared to meet fully even before the pet arrives in your house. You must be made aware of the fact that a bird cannot be neglected, even for a day, without suffering some ill effects which, if the neglect continues for any length of time, will end with the poor creature on the bottom of the cage, feet in the air.

Food is the most important single item in the life of every living thing on this earth, from man to plants. And birds are no exception. Rather, they require more attention to their diet than do many other kinds of animals—dogs, cats, reptiles, and so on.

Also, a dog, cat, or reptile can be made to go without proper food and even water for long periods of time, while a bird cannot survive such treatment. When a person says his friend "eats like a bird," intending to convey the message that the friend is a very light eater, he could not be further from the truth.

Birds eat constantly, throughout their waking hours, and a supply of clean, fresh food must be in front of them at all times. Also, not having a digestive system like man, most birds require some kind of assistance in order to grind up their food. This assistance takes the form of fine gravel, or sand, which is clean and sharp. The birds eat some of this material which aids in grinding up the seeds and other foods they eat.

The gravel which is kept at all times on the bottoms of the cages is not the only gravel which should be supplied to the birds. During the course of the day, this gravel will be contaminated by the bird's own droppings, and the creature may be seen picking in among the grains. It is far better, from the point of view of health and cleanliness, to provide additional grit in a small cup hung from the bars of the cage.

In such a cup may be kept a mixture of two parts clean gravel, four parts crushed oystershell, and one part bird charcoal. When the cup becomes soiled from droppings, it may be emptied and refilled with fresh mixture. Using this mixture the bird is assured of sharp gravel to fill his crop in order to help digest food, oystershell to keep him supplied with calcium, and charcoal to keep the crop from souring.

Clean water is also essential, and this should be placed in cups so designed to protect the water from droppings when the bird sits on a perch above the cup. Finches and Canaries will use a cup attached to the outside of the cage, with a hole leading to the reservoir. The same style cup can be used for seed as well as for water.

Budgerigars do not use this kind of cup to advantage, because these little members of the Parrot family dislike putting their heads through a hole. However, once you have gotten the Budgerigar accustomed to feeding from an outside cup, they seem to have no fear of the opening and will use it as readily as other species of birds. This is especially true of the newer style cups which are square instead of round and have a large square opening in place of the small round opening of the old-style cups.

If the cage you use does not have accommodations for the seed and water cups on the outside, then you should use "hooded" cups inside the cage, placing them in a position protected from the droppings from a perch overhead.

It is useless to try to give a bird anything in a cup placed on the floor of its cage. Within minutes after placing the cup inside, the bird will have overturned it, spilling the contents all over the floor.

The water used for drinking should preferably be boiled for fifteen minutes or so, then put into a clean container to cool to room temperature. If you have only one or two birds, a quart of boiled water will last you up to two weeks, so it is not a great chore to keep a supply on hand.

Water used for bathing purposes need not be boiled, necessarily, but, since there is the possibility of the bird drinking some of its bath water, it is a good idea to use the same treatment that you do for drinking water. It, too, should never be given the bird to bathe in until it is at room temperature. Birdbaths which are fastened to the outsides of cages are available, and these are the best kinds to use.

Lustar Products Company of Springfield, New Jersey, manufactures excellent birdbaths, which fit square or round cages.

Be sure to get the right model for your cage, since the design is slightly different for the two differently shaped cages.

Attention should be paid to the kind of perches in the cage. Plain wooden perches are fine, as are the telescoping plastic ones, ridged for stability. You should never use perches made with a sanded surface. The idea that they afford more traction for the bird's foot is wrong. The bird does not need such traction because of the clamping action of its toes. Then too, the sanded surface abrades the feet of the birds to the point, at times, of even making them bleed. This not only injures the bird but leaves it wide open for infections which could very easily kill it in a very short while.

The same is true of the bottom of the cage. Sandpaper sheets are sold for placing on the bottom, and these have the same danger as a sanded perch. The very best thing to use on the bottom of cages is newspaper. This is also the easiest to maintain. A pad of several sheets of newspaper is torn to fit snugly into the tray. A *small* handful of clean gravel is sprinkled on the paper. Each day, you merely pull out the tray, remove the top sheet of paper and the gravel, shake out any seed and gravel from around the edges of the remaining sheets, replace the handful of gravel with clean material, and return the tray to the cage.

This operation can be done in less time than it took you to read the instructions. And your pet is set for the entire day. The cleaning is best done in the morning, but it could be done in the evening, too, I suppose. The only thing about evening cleanup is that the birds go to sleep as soon as the sun goes down, and you may disturb them.

Saturday night in the author's bird room. The baths fit over the doors of the cages.

For birds like Finches, Canaries, and related birds, toys and gadgets in the cage are only a bothersome clutter, both for you and for the bird. A swing suspended from the top of the cage is all that is necessary, and sometimes a bird will not even use this. The more free room for jumping from perch to perch, with a cage big enough to permit a flutter or short flight, the better your bird will get along. They should have some exercise. And, if you intend to breed them, they *must* have room enough to exercise.

Birds of the hooked-bill group—Parrots, Budgerigars, and others—like a toy or two. The only two I would recommend are a mirror for them to admire themselves in—and, indeed, a Budgerigar can spend hours every day preening himself in front of his mirror—and a small bell, hung from the side or the top of the cage. Possibly, for these inquisitive little pets, a ladder if they are in a large cage and the ladder does not take up too much jumping or flying room. They seem to enjoy hopping up and down the rungs.

Charley, one of our male Budgerigars, will stand for long periods of time on his perch, battering his bell like a boxer smacking a punching bag. Charley does not talk. He was never taught to do so, and by the time we got him, he was too old to train. No matter; he makes up for it by incessantly chattering, especially if we are trying to listen to a television program or music. He enjoys having a duet with a champion Roller Canary, whose song will continue for minutes, unbroken by anything except Charley's raucous gabble.

Budgerigars should have larger cages than Canaries or Finches, since not only do they jump and fly, they climb adroitly. It is an odd sight to see a parrotlike bird—almost all the family do it—walking along the bars of its cage upside

LEFT
A handsome, tall hanging cage on a floor stand.

RIGHT
This cage is huge and will house a large Macaw or Parrot. It can also be used for a Monkey.

down. Or to see it, sitting on its perch, turn clear upside down to pick up a succulent seed from the floor, without even beginning to fall off.

Tall cages are fine for Budgies, while wide cages are better for Canaries. Cages which are large in all dimensions are necessary for the larger birds like Cockatiels, Cockatoos, Macaws, and the big Parrots. Also, it is a good idea to make certain there is a positive latching device on cage doors used for the parrot-family birds, since you will be amazed to see that in a very short time they have mastered the method of opening their door, and you will find them flying about the house.

This cage is suspended on a thin wire hung from the ceiling. The wire is almost invisible, and the cage is at a convenient working level.

There are several ways of protecting your birds in their cages. Remember that a bird in a cage is captive, and it cannot go anywhere except in the relatively small area of the inside of the bars. So use your common sense. Sunlight is an important factor in keeping birds in cages. Direct sunlight can quickly kill a bird if it has no way of getting out of the glare.

Birds can help themselves keep warm a little by fluffing up their feathers to afford more insulation, but they have no way of cooling themselves off when subjected to too much heat. Hence, a bird kept in direct sunlight can suffer sunstroke or heat prostration and, if not removed immediately from the light, will die. Even if it is taken to a shady place, the experience cannot but be harmful and debilitating for the poor creature.

The same thing is true of wind. Birds will get pneumonia from a draft and in a very short time you will have a dead bird on your hands. This is the reason people cover bird cages at night. This is not necessary if you take precaution to see that they are maintained in a draft-free location. Avoid sudden changes. For example, don't open a door in cold weather when the cage is situated where the blast of incoming air will blow right on it. Your birds will not last very long under these conditions.

I do not cover my birds at night, but certain cages are moved from their daytime location to a room where no doors or windows will be opened. They need no protection from ordinary room air movements caused by people walking about. Cages hung near a window are likely to be subject to drafts, too, since practically no window made is entirely free from leaking air. In the summertime, this may not be noticed, but in the winter it is, especially by a bird.

Most small birds are hardier than you may suppose and can be bred in outdoor cages right through the winter in locations not subjected to prolonged subzero weather. One very large bird farm keeps thousands of birds—Canaries, Finches, Budgerigars, and other exotic specimens—in very large walk-in cages, covered with sheet plastic, throughout the entire year. It freezes many nights in winter but warms up a bit during the day, at least above freezing.

Birds purchased from such a dealer can be kept outdoors, but the average bird purchased from a pet store would be dead by morning if it were subjected to these conditions. You cannot take a bird, bred and kept indoors for its entire life, and expect it to survive when placed under "wild" bird conditions. True, the birds bred outdoors are far hardier than those bred indoors, but unless you are interested only in breeding for sale, your pet should be protected from the elements.

In warm climates, a very large outdoor cage is a wonderful break for the birds in summer. They can be turned out there to fly and exercise their wings to their heart's content.

Birds must be kept clean, and they are very willing to perform this service for themselves if they are provided with the proper facilities. A daily bath is very beneficial for Canaries, Budgies, and Finches. Most birds will use a birdbath fastened to the outside of their cage and filled with cool water. Some will not, but will bathe in a shallow dish placed in their cage.

If your bird will not use the bath, sprinkle some water on it and the chances are it will then go into the bath. Sometimes they do not recognize what the bath is for, and they are reluctant to enter what may seem to be a trap.

There may be a mess for you when the bird shakes itself dry, but this is merely one of the things to cope with when you keep a bird. If you are unwilling to do the things necessary for the welfare of your captive, then it is better not to have one.

Messes made by bathing birds can be dealt with, perhaps, by placing the cage with the dish for bathing in the bathtub, closing the shower doors or curtains, and leaving it there until the bird has finished splashing and shaking. Then the cage may be returned to its regular location after drying the bars and changing the paper in the bottom. Morning is the best time to let your birds bathe, since morning is the best time to clean the cage, change the food and water, replace the paper in the bottom, and perform any other chores of maintenance needed. Give the bath water first, then the cleanup you do will perform all servicing at the same time.

This Cockatiel seems to be really enjoying his bath, splashing for several minutes while his mate looks on awaiting her turn.

Different kinds of birds require different kinds of cages. For Canaries, the cage should be not less than 15″ in one dimension, and the higher it is, the better, since this will give the birds room for short flights. Finches are smaller than Canaries and require cages with bars spaced closer together— not more than ⅜″ spacing, or the little Finches will easily slip through. Some Finches, notably Zebra Finches, are smaller than a Wren. They are really tiny, and a standard Canary cage is entirely unsuitable for them.

Budgies will live in Canary cages, but they should have as large a cage as you can get, and no more than one pair kept in one large cage—that is, one male and one female. Two males should not be kept in the same cage unless you want feathers flying about the room, finally resulting in a dead bird. They fight without provocation. Cages for Budgerigars should have horizontal bars, at least on two sides, because Budgies use their bills for climbing, and the horizontal bars act as a ladder, making it easy to get around in the cage. Vertical bars would only let the birds slip and slide to the bottom, and there is the good possibility of their toes catching in the wires and being injured.

For Cockatiels a very large cage is needed. One of the large Parrot cages is fine, and the birds should be kept separately unless you are breeding them. The same kind of large cage is good for a Parrot or a Mynah bird.

Attention should be given to the positioning of the perches. First of all, they should never be placed so the vent of the bird overhangs either the food or the water dishes. Birds, as explained earlier, eat almost constantly. They also make droppings almost constantly, and these should be kept out of their

LEFT
The high, square floor-stand cage is ideal for Finches and Canaries.

RIGHT
Round, tall floor cages are good for Budgerigars, but you should give them a toy ladder to climb on so that they will not slide down the bars.

This is a beautiful floor cage, and it will house a Canary or Budgie very well. The horizontal bars make it perfect for Budgies.

food and water dishes. Next, depending on the kind of bird you are getting, the perches must be placed far enough from the sides of the cages to permit room for the tail feathers to hang free. A perch placed close to the bars of the cage will result in broken and ragged tail feathers, and your bird will always look ruffled and unkempt.

Cages which are to be hung from a bracket, or in a floor stand, in one of the lived-in rooms of the house should have a seed guard of some kind attached to them. These are in the shape of plastic strips wrapped around the cage, or as plastic aprons slipped into guard holders made on the cage itself. The seed and water cups are kept below the top edge of the seed guards, and thus most of the seed scattered by the bird will fall within the cage rather than being shot all over the floor of the room, making a mess that will soon dampen the ardor of a bird lover. Such seed guards will also help keep down the water splashed about when the bird bathes in a dish.

An indoor flight cage belonging to William Holohan of Auburn, Massachusetts. Note the slant of the perch racks to eliminate droppings falling on the birds below.

Often a Canary can be tamed enough so that it will sit on your finger, or perch on your head or shoulder, riding about the room as you move. Budgerigars, too, are easily finger-trained as well as trained to talk. These birds can be let out of their cages for a time each day, or several times a week, and the freedom and extended flight room is very beneficial to them. It is not a good policy, however, to release birds which are not very tame, since the hysteria generated when attempting to return them to their cage is worse for them than the extra freedom is beneficial. Some birds, when tamed enough to be released, will fly about for a time, then, of their own accord, return to their cage for the night. If you have such a pet, thank your lucky stars, and enjoy it.

The claws of perching birds should be clipped about twice a year. They grow long and curved, and sometimes will grow so much as to prohibit the bird from grasping the perch. Regular nail clippers can be used for this service, but you must be careful to avoid injuring the creature.

Each claw in a bird's foot has a vein running part way down it. Most of the time this vein is clearly visible, and the claw is clipped just above the vein. If the vein is severed, it hurts the bird and the foot bleeds—sometimes for a long time. A bird may actually bleed to death through the careless cutting of its claws, although this is not something you need constantly fear. Just make sure you clip off the outer ends of the claws, and you—and the bird—will be all right.

When clipping, the bird should be held completely enclosed in the hand with its wings in a natural folded position, close to the body. The leg is held between two fingers, close to the foot, and care is needed to make sure the bird does not jerk its foot at the instant you clip, or you may clip off a toe! On the other hand, a bird's leg—that of a small cage bird, at least—is a very fragile object, and a rough or hard grip on it can easily break it.

If you are hesitant about the job of clipping, or think you cannot do it properly, then the best thing to do is to take the bird to a veterinarian, or to a pet dealer who knows what to do, or to a friend who knows how to clip them. A very easy way to make sure you are clipping the nail at the proper point is to wear a set of magnifier lenses while doing the job. The kind with lenses of 7″ focal length are the easiest to manage, since with this power you can work at a comfortable distance and still have plenty of room to hold the bird and operate the clipper.

Seeds for Captive Birds

The great majority of birds kept as pets are seedeaters. But some of them are insectivorous, and some of them eat both insects and seeds. Seeds of many kinds are available from companies specializing in pet foods.

On the opposite page is a table of nutritional values, with percentages of protein, fat, and carbohydrates. All hemp seeds available from seed companies have been treated so they will not germinate, to eliminate the possibility of a person buying it as bird food but raising their own marijuana as a side business. The percentages are useful only as a guide as to which seeds are higher in protein or in fat or in carbohydrates. The table does not represent a laboratory analysis. The difference between the combined percentages and 100 per cent represents moisture content.

It is important that the seeds fed to cage birds be fresh. A seed that will not germinate, for example, has little nutritional value. The exception is hemp, or marijuana, of course, which would be capable of germination if it had not been "killed" artificially.

Some seeds should not be given in large quantities, especially the oily seeds which for a captive bird in a small cage would be too fattening. Niger is a particular favorite of almost every bird, and a mixture of several seeds, predominately niger, is given in small cups as a treat to Canaries, Finches, and many other birds. One such small cup a day is plenty. More would be too much. Some breeders only give a treat cup of this mixture to their Canaries once a week.

Seed	Protein	Carb.	Fat
Anise	18	55	12
Buckwheat	10	75	2
Canary	14	70	4
Caraway	22	53	17
Corn	9	75	4
Fennel	16	55	12
Flax	25	22	37
Gold of Pleasure	22	40	30
Hemp	22	40	30
Millet	13	75	3
Milo	12	72	4
Niger	20	30	43
Oats	12	74	5
Peanuts	28	23	36
Poppy	21	22	50
Rape	20	28	45
Rice	8	78	2
Sesame	21	30	47
Spray Millet	15	70	6
Sunflower	15	49	28
Wheat	12	76	2

ANISE (*Pimpinella anisum*) Small oval seeds with ridged husks, and usually with a short piece of the stem attached. There are five ridges on the husk. The seeds are shiny black.

BUCKWHEAT (*Fagopyrum esculentum*) Oval seeds with a high, sharp ridge in the center, making the cross section a triangle. They are brown or gray, and the kernel is black.

CANARY (*Phalaris canariensis*) Tan to brown slender ovals with sharply pointed ends. The kernel is brownish. The hulls split into two halves when the birds eat them, and these hulls fall back into the seed cup, leading you to believe that the bird is not feeding well. It is a good idea to blow the chaff out of the cup, or empty the cup and refill it with fresh seed. Those on the left are shelled, those on the right still have the hulls in place.

CARAWAY (*Carum carvi*) Long, slender, curved seeds, with a ridged surface and a pungent odor. Brown in color. These are also used to flavor rye bread.

CORN (*Zea mays*) Certainly corn should need no description. It is usually fed to birds in the cracked condition, differently sized grains used for differently sized birds. The yellow variety is better than the white.

FENNEL (*Foeniculum vulgare*) A quite large, five-ridged seed, sometimes used in treat mixtures and in Finch mixtures.

FLAX (*Linum usitatissimum*) Brown or yellow in color, the flax seeds are flattened oval, narrower at one end than at the other. In olden times, flax seeds used to be put into the eye in order to remove a cinder or other irritating speck.

GOLD OF PLEASURE (*Camelina sativa*) Gold of Pleasure, sometimes called False Flax, looks very like a miniature grain of wheat. It is high in proteins and fats.

HEMP (*Cannabis sativa*) A large, slightly oval, slightly flattened seed, hard, gray-brown in color. It is useful for larger birds from about the size of cockatiels up, but too much hemp seed in the diet may cause a disorder of the liver. It should be offered sparingly.

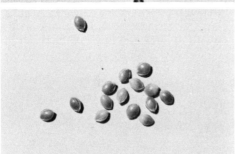

MILLET (*Panicum miliaceum*) Common millet comes in three colors—red, yellow, and white. The white is used in the Budgerigar mix. The red millet is somewhat smaller and is greatly relished by Finches.

MILO (*Andropogon sorghum*) Also caller sorghum, milo is found in several different colors. The ones most used for cage-bird food are white and red. The seeds are round, large, and have no hull or covering.

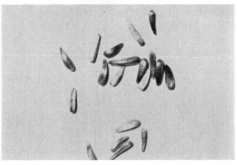

NIGER (*Guizotia abyssinica*) Shiny black, long, narrow, and pointed at the ends, niger is one of the very favorite foods of cage birds, especially Canaries. Niger belongs to the sunflower family, even though many bird fanciers call the seeds thistle.

OATS (*Avena sativa*) Oats, like corn, should need no description. Groats are hulled oats. While most birds love oats, they should be fed sparingly because they are so fattening. Birds in large outdoor aviaries can be fed larger quantities, because they get exercise flying in the cage.

PEANUTS (*Arachis hypogaea*) Large Parrots and even Cockatiels take peanuts with relish. Again, these are very fattening and should be offered in small quantities.

POPPY (*Papaver somniferum*) Poppy is also called Maw and Moan. The seeds are very small, kidney-bean shaped, and come in several colors, the commonest being black and gray. There is no opium in poppy seeds, contrary to popular belief. Poppy is high in protein and fat.

RAPE (*Brassica rapa*) Small, round black seeds belonging to the cabbage family, these form part of the staple diet of Canaries. Some birds will pick out the rape to the exclusion of other seeds, and other birds do not like to eat them at all. Individual taste.

RICE (*Oryza sativa*) Rice is mainly carbohydrate and is used in treat mixtures. For birds which have room for exercise, rice is a beneficial food. These still have the hulls in place

SESAME (*Sesamum indicum*) This familiar seed is used in making candy bars, on the tops of rolls, breadsticks, and cookies as well as being used for bird food. The pale yellowish seeds are oval, flattened, and very slippery.

SPRAY MILLET (*Setaria italica*) Spray millet differs from common millet in being smaller, rougher, and tightly gathered in bunches on long sprays. Most birds love it, and it is helpful to offer a spray once or twice a month to all cage birds.

SUNFLOWER (*Helianthus annuus*) These are delicious seeds, even to humans, and almost all the psittacines love them, too. Other birds, large enough to crack the rather tough hulls to extract the succulent kernels, eat them with relish. Related to niger.

WHEAT (*Triticum vulgare*) Used for larger birds, or, cracked, for Budgerigars and small birds. Wheat is high in carbohydrates and has a moderate amount of protein. Its main benefit is in its vitamin E content.

There are many other seeds used in the feeding of captive birds, but the ones described here are the most common. If you buy the excellent mixes available from seed companies, you need not bother getting individual types of seeds and mixing them yourself. It is better to get seeds from a regular supplier in bulk than to purchase packaged food, and if you have a large number of birds, it is far cheaper to buy in quantity.

As you feed your birds, some seed is discarded each day when you replenish the food cups. This, scattered in the yard, will sprout, and the greens resulting are also excellent food. Especially relished are the tender leaves of the rape seed. They resemble cabbage leaves to a degree, and the birds all love them.

A group of Finches in an aviary at the Canary Bird Farm in Old Bridge, New Jersey.

Breeding Finches and Canaries 4

The breeding season for cage birds, especially Finches and Canaries, extends from about the middle of March to the end of June. Budgerigars and others of the psittacines will breed all the year around if kept indoors in cages, but only during the regular breeding season if kept in outdoor aviaries. Cockatiels will breed indoors whenever you give them a nesting box.

Probably the most important single part of breeding birds is bringing them into breeding condition. This is not just to see that they have seed and water, but they must be given special foods in special quantities, and at certain times, before they are ready to lay and raise a family. The birds must be in breeding condition before they are mated and the hens permitted to make their nests. There are nearly as many recipes for nestling food as there are breeders. I will give you my recipe, which works perfectly for me. It is the recipe given me by William Holohan, a Canary breeder of over thirty-five years' experience. The base of the recipe is English Nestling Food, obtainable from the Hershey Seed Company, 41 North Moore Street, New York, New York 10013. They will ship via mail if desired. The recipe follows:

English Nestling Food . . . 6 tablespoonfuls
Royal Lunch Crackers . . . 2 tablespoonfuls
2 hard-boiled eggs, mashed through a sieve
1½ tablespoonfuls strained carrots

All ingredients are thoroughly mixed together with a fork, then placed in a covered container and kept in the refrigerator. DO NOT USE THIS FOOD AFTER THE SECOND DAY! The reason for this precaution is because the minute you open a hard-boiled egg it begins to spoil, and while you may eat such an egg two or three days later, a Canary cannot eat it without the danger of becoming sick. Chicks can be killed by spoiled food.

The Royal Lunch Crackers used in the recipe are a Nabisco product and can be purchased in almost any grocery store or supermarket. The crackers are rolled into crumbs with a rolling pin before using them in the bird-food recipe. The strained carrots are those which are sold everywhere as human baby food. Strained sweet potatoes may also be used, but the carrots seem to be the best.

If you are breeding only a hen or two, you might cut the recipe to suit your needs. Conversely, if you are breeding a large number of birds, the recipe may be doubled, or increased as many times as necessary, to provide you with a two-day supply. Keep the food mixture refrigerated at all times, removing it to use it, then returning it to the cold immediately. Discard any leftovers at the end of the second day, and make up your new batch the next morning when you are ready to feed the birds.

Beginning about the first of January, the food should be given to each bird, male and female, in a treat cup, once a week. This is continued for the entire month of January. At the end of the month, increase the amount to two treat cups each week for each bird. After the middle of February, the food is given daily from then on until the hen lays her first egg. At this time the conditioning food is stopped until about two days before the eggs hatch, when the food is again offered in a treat cup.

There are three ways commonly used in breeding birds. One is in an outdoor aviary, another in an indoor aviary, and the third in individual cages.

Outdoor-aviary breeding is practiced when quantity is desired, with little or no regard to blood lines or type of stock.

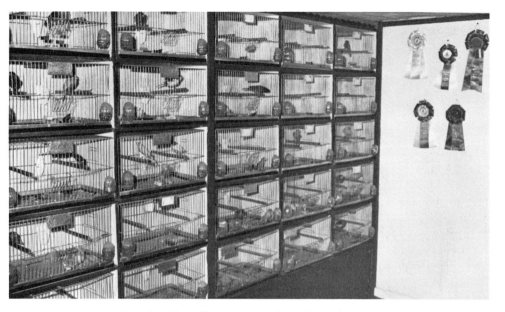

A rack of breeding cages in the aviary of William Holohan, and some of the ribbons his birds have won.

In this method, as many breeding birds as the aviary will accommodate are placed together, nesting boxes or nest baskets hung around the walls, a supply of nesting material placed where the birds can easily locate it, and the birds left to their own devices. It is obvious that with the birds interbreeding, no check can be kept of their parentage. The point is to let the birds breed as freely as they will, and gather the harvest of young ones at the end of the season.

The season is short in the outdoor aviary, one or, at most, two nests being the norm, since the birds wait until warm weather to begin to mate and make their nests; and the spring is well advanced before the first nest is fledged and the hen is ready for her second nest.

Indoor-aviary breeding is almost identical with breeding in an outdoor aviary, with the difference that the birds can be brought into breeding condition much sooner, since the temperature indoors is much warmer than it is outside. Thus the indoor breeder can obtain an extra nest each season, and, if he is breeding many females, this can result in a considerable increase in the number of young obtained in any year.

The serious breeder, however, is reluctant to breed in a community system like this but does his mating and rearing in individual cages, with accurate records kept of all hens and males, as well as the progeny obtained from them.

In this method of breeding birds, exact records may be kept of all adults, blood lines, type, color, or whatever you desire. The young may be family-banded so that their ancestry is known at all times; thus line breeding is possible without getting your stock mixed up. Faults may be bred out of stock, desirable points bred into them, colors fixed or developed; for any kind of breeding, including breeding for song, can be performed in the individual cage.

In this method, also, any hen (or male) which shows undesirable characteristics may be removed in order not to propagate those faults. Often you will find a hen which, while laying full nests of fertile eggs, fails to rear her young properly. Either she does not feed them sufficiently for vigorous growth, or perhaps she does not cover the chicks well enough, permitting them to chill. Such a hen should not be used for breeding. You will only waste time, lose the chicks, and become exasperated with the whole thing. Better to sell her or give her away and use another hen.

Sometimes the male is at fault. Males will sometimes breed very well, and the hen will have healthy chicks. She may feed them well and cover them well, but the male will interfere. Either he will keep chasing her off the nest, or perhaps throw the chicks out of the nest himself. It is often the case that a male will actually pick the chicks to death.

In cage breeding you can watch out for all of these things, where in aviary breeding you will miss most of them, since you cannot possibly watch individual pairs in the aviary the way you can in a breeding cage.

Double breeding cages are by far the best to use, since in these both the hen and the male can be placed at the same time, being kept apart by the screen or solid partition supplied with the cage when you buy it. The hen is placed on one side and the male on the other. The wire partition is the best to use, since this enables both birds to see each other and so become acquainted.

It is not at all uncommon for a pair of birds, on being placed into a breeding cage without a partition, to fight viciously, resulting in the death of one or the other, or at the best, injury and nervous damage to the point where neither bird is of any use for that breeding season.

When the partition is used, food and water cups are, naturally, placed on both sides of the partition for each bird. Then you watch them for several days to see how they get along. If both birds are in fine breeding condition, the male will perhaps begin to feed the female through the bars of the partition. If this is observed, you may without concern withdraw the partition to put the two birds together. It is best to remove the barrier at night, so the birds will find each other at dawn, more or less naturally.

As soon as the partition is withdrawn, the nest should be placed in the cage. Probably the easiest and the best type of nest, especially for Canaries, is the basket or strainer type. These look like nothing more than a large tea strainer without a handle, but with two clips on one side. The strainer is hung over the bars in one end of the cage. Such strainer-type nest baskets are usually supplied with each breeding cage, and, with the double cages, two nests are supplied.

The strainer nest baskets must be lined before the bird can use them. Linings are also sold ready-cut to size and shape, and these liners may be used more than once, by turning them over after the first use and placing them back in the strainer. Since they cost only a few cents each, it is very economical to use the manufactured liners rather than to try to make your own.

The nest liners serve as a soft bed for the chicks, as a support for the hair lining which the bird will make, and, most importantly, to keep the air from chilling the bottoms of the eggs while they are being incubated and the bottoms of the chicks after hatching.

The first day or two after removing the partition, the birds should be observed frequently, to make sure they are really compatible. Particularly important is the mating procedure. Make certain that the hen accepts the attentions of her mate without too much objection. If persistent avoidance of the male's attention takes place, the birds should be separated and the hen tried with another male, and the male given another hen. Of course, they should once again be placed in partitioned cages to do this.

Usually, however, after a pair of birds are introduced through a cage partition, there is no trouble with the mating, and you may continue with the breeding schedule.

Five or six days after removing the partition, the hen should begin picking at the paper or even at the feathers of the male. She is showing a desire to make a nest and is looking for nesting material. At this time you should place a supply of nesting hair in the cage, confined in a small hopper of some kind. Such hoppers are sold at bird suppliers for a few cents, and they last for many years. Goat hair is commonly used for making the nest, and this material is sold in pet stores in small boxes containing a fraction of an ounce per box. One box will supply enough hair for about three nests. Goat hair is also sold by the pound for breeders who are mating a large number of birds.

The hen should begin to line her nest within a day or two after being given the hair. Sometimes—usually, I find—either the hen, the male, or both birds, will pick the hair out of the hopper and scatter it all over the bottom of the cage. I put it back in the hopper once or twice, but if the birds persist in scattering it, leave it alone after that, and let them use it as they will from the cage bottom. If they soil the hair too much, then it is best to remove it and give them a new supply. This is not too great a nuisance, however, since most hens take the hair from the hopper and line the nests with it without too much waiting around.

You will find some hens lining their nests really neatly, tucking the hair in tightly, and making a snug, even lining all around. Others simply pile the hair inside the nest loosely, and when they lay their eggs, get them all tangled up in the loose hair. With such a hen, it is a good practice to wait until she has laid her first egg, then, remove the nest from the cage and the egg from the nest, rub the hair down with your fingers until it is tight against the felt lining, or even work it down with an electric light bulb as a form. The nest is then replaced in the cage.

As the hen lays, each egg is carefully removed from the nest and a clay nest egg, obtainable from pet stores, is substituted. A Canary clutch consists of from three to five eggs, and they lay one egg each day, usually in the morning between 6:00

and 9:00 A.M. A small covered container is used to hold the eggs while the hen is laying, and the lid of the container is labeled accurately with the number of the hen, the date she began to lay, and the cage number if you use that system. The container should be partly filled with birdseed as a bed for the eggs.

This might be a good spot to digress long enough to describe a system of cage labeling that is easy to use and nearly fool-proof. Office-supply stores, department stores, and stationery stores sell labels of many sizes in boxes. These are self-ad-hering, and they come in two types—peelable and permanent. You should use the peelable type, since you will want to be able to remove them from the cages after the breeding is over.

A convenient size to use is ⅜″ by 1¼″, which is a standard size sold in boxes of 1,000 labels for about a dollar. The labels are mounted on sheets of glazed paper from which they are easily peeled for use. Leaving the labels on the sheet, I use a felt marking bottle to color code them. Running the bottle down the rows of labels, I color one half of each label, leaving the other half uncolored. I use a four-color code system for breeding and mark a full sheet of labels with each color. These are then ready for use as follows. My code is this:

Blue for laying hens
Yellow for incubating hens
Green for setting hens
Red for hens with hatched chicks

You may use whatever colors you like, naturally, but what-ever code you use should be placed on a file card, and this card pinned in a convenient location in your breeding room.

The full clutch has been returned to the nest and incubation will now begin. The chicks will all hatch the same day.

Canary eggs are unbelievably fragile, and if you pick them up by your fingertips, I can almost guarantee you will squash them. Rather, use a spoon, bent into a scoop, or, if you *do* use your fingers, roll the egg partly up the side of the nest, then let it roll down your fingers into your hand without putting any gripping pressure on the egg itself. Tip it gently out of your fingers into the birdseed in the container, but do not let it *fall* into the seed, or the side of the shell hitting the seed will crack or cave in.

The eggs are removed daily as they are laid, and the nest eggs substituted for them until the fourth egg has been laid. Sometimes a hen will lay only three eggs. You will know she is not going to lay any more if one day elapses without an egg being laid. In other words, she will lay an egg a day for three days, and the fourth morning no egg will appear. When this happens—which is by no means unusual—you may assume that she has completed her clutch.

Now, when the first egg appears, I take a blue label and stick it on the frame of the cage, writing in the date the first egg was laid. When she has completed her clutch and is given her own eggs back, a yellow label is fastened *over* the blue one, and the date on the yellow label is *seven days after the eggs are returned to the hen*. This is the date the eggs are to be candled. More about candling later.

When the fourth egg appears, or, as just mentioned, the fourth morning with only three eggs, the clay nest eggs are taken from the nest and the genuine eggs returned to the hen. She will begin to set them, and all her eggs will hatch on the same day, or, at the most in two days for the entire clutch. It is best to give the hen back her own eggs in the morning.

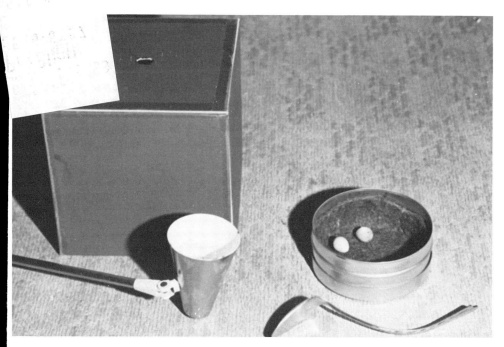

A candler made out of cardboard, using a high-intensity lamp, is all you need to test your eggs for fertility.

Let us interrupt again to tell you about the candling of eggs. Candling is nothing more than looking inside an egg to see if it is fertile and developing into a chick. It is the easiest thing in the world to do, but remember the fragility of the tiny eggs, and handle them accordingly. Actually, all you need for candling is a flashlight, turned on and placed on a table, so you can hold the egg in front of the ray to look through the shell. It is much more accurate and easy if you use some method of blanking out the light around the egg, to concentrate the light through the egg itself.

A candler can be made with squares of cardboard and masking tape. Five squares are cut, and four of them taped together to make a box. The fifth is then taped to the other four, to close one end of the box. Into this square a small hole is cut with a sharp knife or heavy shears. The hole must be smaller than an egg so it will not fall through. The size of the box is unimportant. It can be anywhere from 5 to 6 inches square, and deep enough to accommodate whatever light you intend using. One of the small high-intensity lamps is perfect for a candler, but a flashlight will also serve. In use, the light is turned on and the box placed over it, positioned so the hole is directly above the light beam. Now an egg placed over the hole will appear almost transparent to the eye, and you can very readily observe the yolk and the white inside.

If the inside of the egg shows any darkening or any color other than the tiny yolk floating in a clear fluid, you may assume that the egg is fertile. If, on the seventh day after the hen has set her eggs, the yolk is still clearly defined, the egg is infertile and should be discarded.

After the eggs are candled, if they are fertile, a green label is stuck over the yellow label, and the date on this label is *fourteen days after the hen was set on the eggs.* This is the date the eggs are due to hatch.

On the morning of the fourteenth day you should gently nudge the hen off her nest to see if the eggs did hatch. Sometimes they do not hatch until the evening of the fourteenth day, and often will carry over, or at least one or two eggs will carry over to the next morning. In any event, when the chicks hatch, the red label is fastened over the green one, and the date the *last* chick hatched is placed on this space.

A Canary hen can lay eggs for a considerable length of time without debilitating herself. She may also set eggs with no ill effects. It is the rearing and feeding of the chicks that wears her down, which is the reason for limiting the number of nests you take from a hen each season.

Since the laying and the setting of the eggs does not wear her out, you candle the eggs to determine fertility. If the eggs are fertile, you return them to the nest and the hen continues to set them. It is at this time you fasten the green label with the hatching date—fourteen days—written on it. If the eggs are infertile, you remove them and the nest. Then you either remove the male, leaving the hen alone in her breeding cage, or place the hen in a flight cage for about one week. The hen is then put back into the breeding cage, the male placed beyond the partition for a day or two, then the partition removed, the nest placed in the cage, and the cycle begun all over again.

If a hen deposits two nests of infertile eggs, the chances are she and the male are not compatible. In this case she should be introduced to a different male. Likewise, the male can be given a new hen in another cage.

After the chicks are hatched, the hen is kept supplied with the nestling food at all times until dusk, when the food remaining in the cup is removed from the cage. A regular feeding schedule should be established for hens with chicks, and, while it is a bit of trouble, and you will lose a little sleep over it, still, in the best interest of the growing birds you must follow it.

The first feeding should be as close to dawn as possible. You may have to set the alarm clock in order to get up then but the feeding takes only a couple of minutes, then you can go back to bed.

A busy mother Canary feeding four hungry chicks.

The feeding schedule is as follows: First feeding at dawn. The food cup is partly filled and placed inside the cage, then leave the birds alone while you go back to bed. The next feeding is around nine o'clock in the morning. The food cup should be empty or nearly empty by then. At this second feeding, I sprinkle three or four drops of wheat-germ oil into each food cup right on top of the nestling food. This seems quite beneficial to the birds, and you may do the same if you wish.

Wheat-germ oil is obtainable from the Hershey Seed Company, or from health-food stores. Never leave food in the cup during subsequent feedings. Empty out the stale food and put in fresh. Remember that baby birds need no great amount of food, so do not heap the cup full. Only partly fill it. One or two feedings should tell you the right amount to give them. Around one or two o'clock the birds should have their third feeding, and the last feeding about four in the afternoon. This food is left in the cage until dusk, when the cup is removed from the cage; the paper on the bottom of the cage is also removed, and fresh gravel is sprinkled on the fresh paper.

The removal of the paper is most important, and the reason is that, during the day, in feeding her chicks the hen will scatter particles of food all around the bottom of the cage. This food will spoil, especially during the hot days, and if the paper is not removed at early dawn, before you get to the first feeding, she will pick up this food and feed the chicks with it, usually killing them in the process with food poisoning. We lost several nests of babies because of this problem before we discovered what was wrong. Since the method of paper changing was put into operation, the infant-mortality rate dropped to zero. It is well worth the trouble, since the entire operation of changing paper and gravel takes not more than a minute.

About sixteen to eighteen days after the chicks are hatched, the hen will be ready to make a second nest. At this time, both the hen and the male should be partitioned off in the end of the cage opposite the one containing the old nest and the babies. The parent birds will continue to feed their chicks through the bars of the partition.

If the chicks are left with the adult birds at the time of the second nesting, there is a better than good chance that the hen will pull the feathers out of the chicks to line her new nest. Partitioning them off eliminates this possibility, and the hen will make her new nest in the usual manner, provided you supply her with fresh nesting hair and another nest.

At the time of partitioning off, a small dish of nestling food should be placed on the floor of the cage on the chicks' side, in addition to the regular supply given the hen. The baby birds will soon learn to eat this by themselves. When you see them picking at the nestling food, you can sprinkle a small quantity of regular seed on the floor of their cage, or even better, a shallow jar lid containing seed may be placed on the floor where the young birds may find it easily. After a few days the seeds may be put into a treat cup, mixed with the nestling food.

When the chicks are from twenty-one to twenty-three days old, they should be picking seed for themselves and can then be removed from the breeding cage to a small cage of their

Canary chicks, one hour, two days, and three weeks old.

own. They should be closely watched for several days, to make sure they are feeding properly. If a chick peeps constantly in a plaintive tone, it is crying for food and is unable to fend for itself. A young chick will literally stand ankle deep in food and yet starve to death, simply because it does not know enough to feed itself. If the chick does peep without letup after removal to its own cage, it must be replaced with the hen for another day or two, for further instruction in feeding. Then it can again be transferred to its hardening cage.

After the chicks have been in their own small cage for a week, they are transferred to a large flight cage. They may be left in this cage for the remainder of the year, or they may be taken from the flight cage to individual cages after they have been in the flight cage for about a month.

While in their own cage and while in the flight cage, the nestling food, mixed with seed, is fed to them. Seed cups are also kept supplied, along with the shallow lid of seed on the floor. When finally you see them eating seed several times during the day, you may start cutting down on the amount of nestling food and increase the amount of seed in proportion until they are weaned entirely to the seed. This should take from three weeks to a month. When the birds are about six to seven weeks old, they should be given greens daily the same as the adults, and from then on their diet is the same as that of the adult birds.

Close observation of the young birds in the flight cage should tell you which of them are males. From one month to five weeks old, the young chicks make attempts to sing if they are males. They go through all the motions, mouth open, tongue moving, and throat vibrating, but no sound is heard. They

Large flight cages in the author's bird room, used for breeding Budgerigars.

cannot yet produce notes but can only exercise their singing apparatus. When a bird is observed going through these motions, it is almost certain that it is a male. They can then be color-banded, or some other method of identification can be used, to help you identify them when the time comes to segregate males from females.

About August the birds go into their first molt, and it is then almost impossible to sex them. During this time, a good molting food, also obtainable from Hershey Company, should be given them daily in addition to their regular diet of seed.

About the only important difference between breeding Canaries and breeding other types of Finches is that the Finches prefer a closed nesting box to the open-basket-type nest used for Canaries. It is just as important to bring your Finches into breeding condition and to supply them with the proper diet.

A baby Finch a couple of hours old. The grass nest is made in a
Budgie box.

A Lady Gould Finch. One of the most spectacular birds obtainable.

When breeding the gorgeous Lady Gould Finches, you should use a somewhat different approach. Among the big problems with this species is that they do not incubate very well in cages, and they do not take very good care of their young. For this reason, Lady Goulds are usually fostered out to other species of Finches—mainly Society Finches. These interesting birds are probably the easiest of all birds to breed. They mate readily, either in individual cages or in community in an aviary. They will accept eggs from other hens and hatch them. They will feed their young with no trouble and will also feed other hens' young if community bred.

When attempting to breed Lady Gould Finches, you should condition at least one or two pairs of Society Finches simultaneously with the Goulds. When the Gould hen lays her eggs, they are removed from the nest and placed under a Society hen. This bird will hatch them and rear the young as if they were her own. However, there is one hazard that must be understood and taken into consideration when using Society Finches as foster parents for Gouldian chicks. Society Finches mature a few days earlier than do the young Gouldians, and, if not watched carefully, the female will desert the fledglings before they are able to feed for themselves, in order to start her second nest.

This trouble may be overcome by removing the female when she shows the first signs of wanting to nest again. Leave the *male* with the young, and he will continue to feed them as long as necessary.

The Lady Gould Finch is probably the most colorful of all the Finches. Certainly it is striking in its vivid, gaudy coat. The head and cheeks are deep red to maroon, the throat black. The nape and collar are pale aquamarine and the back green. The chest is purple to violet and the abdomen deep yellow, fading to white at the far rear end. The tail is black, blue, and gray. Altogether the color scheme is little short of unbelievable, yet on the bird everything blends in to make this creature a prize among the cage birds.

Their coloring, together with the challenge in breeding, taken with their high cost to begin with, makes this Finch a coveted species, and one that is in constant demand. Unfortunately, Lady Goulds have another habit which dampens the ardor of many breeders. For no apparent reason whatever, one of these beautiful birds will suddenly fall off its perch, dead as the proverbial mackerel. As though they sit in their cage, bored with their existence, thinking to themselves, "Ho hum, there's nothing at all to do; I think I'll die!" Plop! When you consider that these Finches cost from $75 to $80 or more a pair, that plop hurts!

There are three recognized varieties of Lady Gould Finches, two of them occurring in the wild. These are the red-faced and the black-faced. The third, the yellow-faced, is found only in captivity and appears to be a cultivated sport. The species is indigenous to Australia.

The diet of Gouldian Finches should be kept simple instead of giving them a pampering selection. A standard Finch mixture of seeds, with a little extra-small yellow millet, is excellent. In addition, spray millet should be offered, and a supply of this kept before the birds at all times. Canary treat can be offered in a small treat cup, as a daily addition, and greens can be fed to them daily as well. A cuttlebone must be fastened inside the cage, and a small cup of grit kept filled. The grit can be the mixture of crushed oystershell, charcoal, and gravel used for almost all cage birds.

In the summer, heads of seeding grasses are welcomed and beneficial to the birds. Dandelion greens, cabbage, almost any table green should be offered daily; and fruit such as sweet red apple, pear, a cherry or grape, or a section of sweet orange makes a good biweekly supplement. Too much rich food causes liver disorders, and it is very possible that improper diet is one of the governing causes of their often sudden death.

Society Finches are not nearly as colorful as the Gouldians, but they are very interesting birds in their own right and, besides, are the ideal foster parents for the more temperamental species; so no bird fancier interested in rearing Finches should be without two or three pair. The price of Society Finches is nearly as low as that of Zebra Finches; therefore, the purchase of a couple of pair should not drain your resources very much.

Society Finches come in many different degrees of color. I say degrees because some are all white with dark markings. Some are pure white. Others have from a very little amount of black or brown mottling to, at times, so much as to appear all black or all brown, with a few white flecks in the feathers.

While they do not sing, as do Canaries and Siskins, they do have a cheerful chirp. Society Finches are unknown in the wild, and their ancestry is also unknown. They have been bred through so many stages of hybridization throughout the centuries, by the Chinese, that it is no longer certain what the parent stock was. Strictly speaking, Societies are not true Finches, but rather belong to that group called Mannikins. True, Mannikins are Finches, but that name has been attached to include some of the Finches as well as some of the Waxbills as a separate classification.

Society Finches. They are used as host parents for the Lady Gould Finches, which do not care for their young very well in captivity.

These little birds prefer the wicker-basket-type nests or wooden nest boxes, such as are used for the Gouldians, to the open Canary nests.

They will nest as readily in a small cage as in an aviary. They are brought into breeding condition by a substantial diet of nutritious foods just as are Canaries. The incubation period is the same as for Canaries—thirteen days—and they will nest any time of the year.

Everything said about Society Finches can be said about Zebra Finches. They are considered the easiest of all the Finches to breed, although I think both species are about equal in this respect. However, Zebra Finches are just a little unpredictable as foster parents, so it is best to breed them for their own species rather than as fosters for Gouldians.

Zebra Finches are more nervous than most other Finches, and they are considerably smaller than the other popular species. They are very fond of spray millet, and when this is offered to them, it has been my experience that they will eat the entire spray before going back to their regular seed cup.

Basket nests are preferred to box nests, but they will accept a box if nothing more is available to them. The box should be partly filled with dry grass or other nesting filler before the Finches use it. They will hollow out the cavity and line it with nesting hair, grass, shredded burlap, or any other material available. Four- to six-inch squares of burlap, hung on the side of the cage with a safety pin, will be carefully pulled apart and the strands used to line the nest.

The eggs are tiny, white, and very fragile. Both birds incubate them, and both male and female will sleep together in the nest. The incubation time for the eggs is about twelve days. No special diet need be offered; their regular diet of Finch mixture seeds is sufficient for their continued well-being.

Zebra Finches mutate frequently, and at least two different strains have become fixed as definite varieties. White Zebras are very pretty, solid dazzling white birds, with deep orange legs and bill. The males have redder beaks than do the females. Gray Zebras are another fixed strain that is very popular. There are several other strains, but these are variations in marking or coloring, and they are rather rare. Some work is being done in England to standardize the different color strains of the Zebra Finch and to arrive at a standard classification for the different mutant species.

The male Zebra Finch has a pretty cheek patch. It is a tiny bird and must have closely spaced bars on its cage.

The next most popular species of Finch is the Ribbon Finch, also known by the unfortunate name of Cutthroat Finch, taken from the fact that the bird carries a narrow band of vivid red across its throat.

While Ribbon Finches are fairly easy to breed, they do not approach the ease of either the Zebra or the Society Finches in this respect. They require a larger cage for breeding than do the other two species just mentioned. One of the standard flight cages, about 21″ deep, 26″ high, and 30″ wide, is obtainable from any of the cage manufacturers and will serve for quarters for two to three pairs of Ribbons. Basket nests should be provided, and the birds should be permitted to pair up and select the nest to their liking. You should place one more nest than you have pairs of birds in the cage, to eliminate any source of rivalry and fighting over their nesting site.

The diet for Ribbon Finches is the same as that used for Societies and most other Finches. No special conditioning foods need be provided, but a cuttlebone and a supply of crushed oystershell, mixed with gravel and charcoal, must be in the cage at all times.

Many breeders claim that the use of oystershell in breeding cage birds accounts for a great number of dead-in-shell chicks. The contention being that too much oystershell makes the birds lay eggs with shells so hard that the tiny chick cannot crack its way out when hatching time arrives. I personally have not had this trouble, and each cage in my bird room has a cup of this material in it. This is not to say that there is no merit to the idea. It is entirely possible that some birds can assimilate calcium from the shell in larger amounts, passing it on in the shells of their own eggs, and that, if this be the case, those eggs may be too tough for the little chick to peck

A male Ribbon Finch. Note the band of dark red color across the throat.

The female Ribbon Finch does not have the red band.

open. This is one of the breeding hints that must be worked out by each individual person. I think the oystershell is of too great a value to eliminate its use, and as long as my chicks are able to peck out, I shall use it.

Many other species of Finches are known to breeders in this country. The more beautiful, both as to color and shape, are the Australian species. Several African species are also bred. With the present embargo on imported birds, these colorful and interesting birds are becoming more and more scarce and will continue to do so until the breeders in this country who already had a supply in stock have managed to breed enough to put them back in the market.

It seems as though Australia was especially fortunate in its population of colorful birds. Besides the Finches, Budgerigars, Cockatiels, and other extremely beautiful psittacines come from that country. To the dismay of the bird fanciers, Australia placed a ban on the exportation of their birds long before our own Department of Agriculture banned birds from coming into the United States, although for a different reason.

Such quantities of birds were being trapped and sent out of the country that the Australian authorities decided it was time to put a stop to the practice while they still had a bird population.

In one way, all this restriction on obtaining wild-caught stock is for the better, since it makes the breeders learn more about how to propagate the stock they already have. This in turn teaches breeders more and more about their species, and the end result is a wealth of knowledge that otherwise would not have been discovered, or, at any rate, would have taken far longer to discover, since the incentive was lacking. The birds also benefit from the increased awareness of their needs, and they breed more freely, thereby increasing the stock in the country and making rare species available to many instead of only to zoos and aviaries.

Besides the species already mentioned, the Crimson or Australian Fire Finch is fairly popular. This is an aggressive bird, though, and should be kept in a large outdoor aviary with no other species present.

Other species are: the Owl Finch, so named because its feather marking strongly resembles the face of an Owl, and the Cherry Finch, a brown-and-plum-colored bird with a little white and metallic green on the body. Some of the Parrot Finches, such as the Pin-tailed Nonpareil, offer a challenge to the American breeder because of their reluctance to accept the diet available in captivity. The Red-headed Parrot Finch is very rare and very high priced. It is also difficult for the beginner to breed, and if you were fortunate enough to obtain a pair of them, you should practice on other birds before trying to produce young from this species. Several aviaries have bred them and there are a few birds on the market that are the result of these endeavors.

The Mannikins are hardy and easy to keep in cages or aviaries, and many species are regularly bred in this country. The Society Finch, of course, is the prime example of the easy-breeding Mannikin. The Spice Finch, from India, is often a pest in its native habitat, where it feeds on rice in the paddies, to the great annoyance of the rice farmers.

Nuns are birds so named because of the black head and shoulder markings, resembling the cape of the religious orders.

There are several species of Nuns known to bird fanciers, and some of them are usually available in this country.

Another group of birds which are classed together with the Finches are the Waxbills from Africa. Actually, the random classification of many of these small birds as Finches is improper. They could, if the need arose for grouping together, all be called soft-billed birds, or, simply, soft bills.

The Waxbills are characterized by having short, heavy bills, glossy, and, for the most part, brilliantly colored. Waxbills require some live insect food, especially during their breeding time. Mealworms, crickets, small grasshoppers, aphids, flies, fly maggots—called "gentles" in England and Europe—white worms, all are good for these sprightly birds, and a diet containing a generous supply of any of the above will help insure a successful breeding season.

The birds called Strawberry Finches are really either the Indian or the Oriental Strawberry Waxbill. They are pretty little birds, colored very like a strawberry, with pickings in the feathers that look like the seeds.

The African Fire Finch is sometimes called the Ruddy Waxbill. These birds are not as hysterical as some of the other Finches and Waxbills, but they do prefer a large aviary to a small cage. They become quite well acclimated if the aviary is well planted and situated in a place to their liking. In the warmer areas of the United States some breeders liberate the birds, leaving an access door open to the aviary and placing the food inside. The birds fly free during the day, seldom straying from the immediate vicinity of the cage, returning to it to feed and roost for the night. They even will nest in the shrubbery outside the aviary.

Of all the Waxbills, the second only to the Lady Gould Finch, both in popularity and in price, are the Cordon Bleus. They are also an African bird, and up to last year many thousands were imported each year. Now there are no more coming in, and the price has gone up accordingly. As with the Lady Gould, the Cordon Bleu is difficult to breed. Perhaps I should say erratic rather than difficult, since if you have success with a pair, you can usually obtain several nests without difficulty.

One thing they require is plenty of insects and live food in their diet. Some of this food is needed at all times, but especially when they are breeding. At that time the insect offering should be increased. Cordon Bleus will breed in a very large cage or aviary, and a good number of plants should be placed inside, even in the cage, where the plants may be potted for ease in handling and care.

Use either Finch nesting boxes or the basket type of Finch nest, and keep the birds alone—that is, no other species than the Cordon Bleu should be put into a cage at the same time. The birds also do not thrive when the breeder disturbs them during the cycle. It is best to perform only the required maintenance in the cage and then leave the birds to their own devices during the entire breeding season.

The last of the Waxbills—but by no means the last of the group—that we will mention here is the Orange-breasted, or Gold-breasted. These are tiny birds, about the size of our domestic Wren. Nervous and constantly on the move, they will fly in and out of a regular Canary cage as though there were no bars present.

For those who are fortunate enough to have room outdoors for a large aviary or protected cage, the African Whydahs are ideal birds, and a challenge to the breeder. While they become well acclimated and thrive in captivity, they are difficult to induce to breed. This is partly due to the fact that some of the species are parasitic upon other birds. Parasitic means that they do not make a nest of their own, but lay their eggs in the nests of other birds, then abandon them to the foster parent—all unwittingly, of course—to rear. Not all of the Whydahs are parasitic, but, unfortunately, the ones most popular are.

In the wild, each species of Whydah parasitizes one particular kind of bird, mainly Finches. And to have any kind of success in breeding Whydahs, you are forced also to maintain and breed those hosts. Since some of the host birds are far more rare and costly than the Whydah, it places somewhat of a burden on the breeder. However, the fact that it is so difficult to do is incentive enough for some people to go to almost any length to achieve success in breeding these most unusual and interesting creatures.

Whydahs resemble Birds of Paradise in that the males, during the courting and breeding season, have enormously long tails. So long, in fact, that they cannot be kept comfortably in anything other than a high, large aviary. During the other times of the year—out of breeding season, that is—the males are drab in appearance and lose their long tail feathers. At this time they are really nothing much to look at, but if you ever see some of the Whydahs in full breeding color and display, you will be hopelessly committed to try to do something with them.

Paradoxically, while Whydahs are nearly impossible to breed in captivity, they take to aviary life readily, are hardy, and seem to be perfectly contented in a captive state. They feed readily, too, and their diet is simple—standard Finch seed mixture, with greens offered daily, and some insect food such as mealworms, crickets, grasshoppers, and the like. If you do attempt to breed them, live insect food should be increased during the breeding season.

An attempt at breeding Whydahs should be well planned before you make any move toward getting your birds. First, the host birds must be identified and obtained, established in the aviary, and permitted to become acclimated. Then the Whydahs can be admitted to their future home and, hopefully, will perform their natural functions, but don't bank on it—at least during the first season.

The breeding of Whydahs is merely a challenge rather than as a profitable occupation, since most Whydahs are not very costly. That is, up to the year 1972. It was that year that the embargo went into effect on importation, and I am sure that the Whydah population in the United States is not nearly large enough to meet the demand. Almost undoubtedly the prices will jump.

I offer a list of some Whydah species and their host birds. Bear in mind that there is every possibility that other birds than the ones listed might act as hosts in the wild, so it would not be a bad idea to put in pairs of several different kinds of Finches when attempting Whydah breeding.

Paradise Whydah.   Host bird—Melba Finch.
Pintailed Whydah.   Host bird—St. Helena Waxbill.
Senegal Combassou.   Host birds—Fire Finch and Cordon
                              Bleu.

Some of the Finches that would be good to use as possible hosts are the Society Finch, Zebra Finch, Violet-eared Waxbill, Orange-breasted Waxbill, Silverbill, and any other species you might find in pet stores or from other breeders. It will not hurt to have as many different species as you can.

The diet for Lovebirds, Budgies, and Cockatiels is Budgie mix, sunflower seeds, greens offered daily, fruit a couple of times each week, and a cuttlebone kept always in the cage, as well as grit and crushed eggshell, or crushed oystershell. A small amount of avian charcoal mixed with the shell and grit is beneficial and will help sweeten the crop.

While it is easy enough to breed the parrotlike birds in captivity, certain things must be done in order to achieve success. One of the most important conditions in successfully raising chicks is sufficient humidity during laying and nesting periods. The eggs of the psittacines harden if the shells dry out, and if this happens the weak chicks are unable to peck open the shells from within.

Many methods have been resorted to in an attempt to prevent this during the hot, dry months. Some of them work; others fail. Yet every method will work for some breeder at some time or other; so a method should not be discarded just because you had no success with it the first or second time you tried it.

Dampened wood shavings are used with good results by some breeders and sworn at by others. It has been my experience that, in the case of Budgerigars, at least, the birds spend more time throwing out every single shaving than they do laying eggs or setting them.

A piece of blotting paper cut to fit under the nest block, and kept moistened by a strip laid as a wick, is also favored by certain breeders. Of course, if you can afford to keep a humidifier in the breeding room, it would be the simple answer to the humidity problem. However, unless you are breeding top-quality birds which can command a high price, it would take a great number of chicks to pay for this piece of equipment.

One or two pails of water placed in the bird room where the birds cannot get to them will help a great deal to keep the air moist. The water should be replenished as it evaporates.

Budgerigars used to sell for three or four dollars in pet stores, with breeders running up as high as fifteen dollars or a bit more. I am afraid those days are gone forever because now young birds, which are nothing really more than cull stock, bring anywhere from eight to twelve dollars each, and a good breeder bird will bring whatever the owner can ask for it. It is not at all uncommon to pay a couple of hundred dollars for a good pair of birds, and there are records of exceptionally fine breeders selling for as high as one thousand dollars! This is out of my class entirely, but I do believe that you should purchase the very finest breeder birds you can afford if it is your intention to rear good stock.

I mentioned before about colony breeding for quantity of birds and individual breeding for quality of birds. If you are breeding to get as many birds as you possibly can, then trying to obtain the finest breeders possible is both a waste of time and money, since birds bred indiscriminately in colony simply *must* deteriorate in blood line and quality. Since most pet stores and pet-store customers are interested only in having a bird as a pet—preferably a tamed, or talking bird—colony breeding is the answer to supplying the market.

However, the true bird fancier is interested in the top quality of his stock and in exhibiting his birds in order to win ribbons and trophies, and here is where the breeding blood lines are so important. Unlike the soft-billed birds, Budgies will breed indoors all year, and so it is possible to find breeding stock at any time of the year, instead of only in a particular season, as with Canaries and Finches.

A box is used for the nesting site, and the standard Budgerigar box measures about 6″ by 10″ high. It is made out of ¼″ plywood, with a ½″ lumber top and bottom. The front and back are nailed to the top and the bottom, and the sides, made of ⅛″ masonite, slide in grooves cut into the plywood front and back, which project out from the top and bottom about ¾″ to permit the sides to be installed. A ½″-diameter hole is drilled through each side, and two through the back, about 2½″ down from the top of the box. These provide ventilation. The hole for the birds to use, going in and out of the nest, is about 2″ in diameter, centered 3″ down from the top of the box, and a ½″-diameter perch is fastened about one inch below the opening to the nest. The easiest way to fasten the perch is to drill a ½″ hole and push a piece of dowel through to project an inch or two inside the nest box, and 3″ outside.

The nesting block is placed in the bottom of the box. This is a square of one-inch pine cut to fit snugly inside when the sides are in place. The block is scooped out to make a shallow depression in the center. This may be done with a gouge or on a lathe if you are making your own boxes, but Budgie nest boxes are so cheap that it hardly pays to make them yourself. The depression in the bottom block resembles the rounded-out hole in a tree. More importantly, though, it serves to keep the eggs rolled all together in the center of the block, to be more easily covered by the hen when she sets them.

Some breeders say to put shavings inside the nest box. Others advocate sawdust. Still others offer dry grasses to their nesting Budgies. I find that usually Budgies will toss out everything you put inside their box, laying their eggs on the bare wooden bottom and raising the chicks there as well.

Breeding condition in Budgies is fairly easy to tell. First of all, you must have mature birds to mate and lay fertile eggs. Young Budgies have barred feathers covering the head and forehead. When a Budgie is adult, these barrings recede to leave the forehead and top of the head solid in color. Surrounding the nostrils is a bare patch of skin called the cere. In adult male Budgies this cere is blue, and in adult females, brown or gray. When the bird is in breeding condition, the female cere is a deep, rich brown and that of the male is a deep, bright blue.

The sexes should be kept in separate flight cages until mating time. When the males strut about the cage and rattle their beaks against the bars, or the feeding cups, and when the females keep calling the males, it is time to put a pair together.

If the nesting box is hung on the outside of the cage, a single breeding cage is plenty large enough to take the pair of birds. The pair should be watched closely the first few days after putting them together. If they fight, of course, they should be separated and paired with other birds. If they show no sign of mating after several days, they could be separated and the hen given to another cock, and vice versa. Best results seem to be accomplished when either the hen or the cock is older than the other. For example, it is better to mate a one-year-old hen with a two-year-old cock than to try mating two one-year-olds.

Budgies apparently resent interference while breeding. Interference by the breeder, I mean. Constantly looking into the nest box is apt to cause the hen to abandon her eggs. It is better

This ugly little Budgie chick has hatched four days before the next egg. He will have all his feathers by the time the last egg has hatched.

to leave the birds alone as much as possible, watching to see other signs of laying. A large pile of droppings is almost a sure sign that she has begun to lay.

Budgies lay an egg every other day until the clutch is completed with from four to seven eggs. They begin to sit on the eggs after the second or third is laid. When the chicks hatch out, there is, of course, the same lapse of a day between hatchings, which means, that with a clutch of six eggs, the first chick will be twelve days old when the last chick comes out of the shell. As soon as you find that the hen has laid the first egg, stop looking into the nesting box because every time you open the box to look, the hen throws a fit and thrashes around inside in a mad scramble to get out of the hole. Usually in doing so, she stamps all over the eggs, puncturing them with her toes. It is better to note the date you saw the first egg in the nest, then in about two weeks you may start listening outside the box. When the chicks hatch, you will hear them peeping as they are being fed by the parents. This is when you start watching the nest. At least every two days look inside— a quick peep, to make sure that none of the chicks have died. They must be removed immediately or they will spoil, and possibly the decomposed matter will kill the other birds.

When all the chicks have hatched, again stop looking into the nest for five or six days. At that time, you take the chicks out to band them, returning them immediately, and leaving them alone for another two weeks, when you may begin to handle them.

Most writers will say that the chicks should be closely examined each day after hatching, and if signs appear that they are not being fed well enough, they should be taken from their parents and given to a foster hen to rear. This is fine, provided you have an unlimited number of Budgerigars, all in breeding condition and all ready to have chicks. If a pair of birds has no chicks of their own, there is no use giving another hen's chicks to them to rear, since they will not accept them. If a hen has chicks of her own, she has enough to do to rear them without adding to her burden by dumping another nest on her.

Many of the same breeders advocate using poor quality, or at least, lesser quality birds than your "good" breeders as the foster parents, throwing out their eggs as they are laid, replacing them with the eggs from the better quality birds. This does not seem like a practical practice to me at all. It takes exactly as much time, as much trouble, and as much expense to rear and feed a bad bird as it does to rear and feed a good bird. Why then, waste all that time, trouble, and expense keeping stock you have no use for in the off chance that a pair will be in the same condition at the same time as a pair of your regular fine-breeding stock?

It is far more practical to try to foster out your chicks among other pairs of good stock, I should think, or, if this is not possible, then let the birds do whatever they are going to do anyway, and be glad of what chicks you end up with. A pair which persistently refuses to feed or care for their chicks should be culled out of your bird room. You should certainly not try to keep them as breeding stock.

A much better way to rear Budgies, in my opinion, is to let them nest as they will, and keep yourself from disturbing them as much as possible after the chicks hatch. About seven or eight days after hatching you can remove them from the nest to band them if you wish, and, at the same time you can clean up the nesting block, which by this time should be pretty dirty. Then return the chicks, close the box, and leave them alone. The hen will provide whatever care the chicks require.

Chicks will die for no apparent reason. Perhaps the hen did not cover them well enough, and one got chilled. If this happens, the food given to the tiny creature will not digest properly, and the bird will die of malnutrition even with a full stomach. Or a chill will give it a cold which ends up with the same result. The other chicks in the nest, having been kept warm by their mother, do not suffer the same calamity.

After the chicks have hatched, you can change the nest block for a clean one, and now you will be able to put in a small handful of cedar chips. These will absorb the liquid droppings of the baby birds and help keep the nesting box clean. The shavings can be renewed every couple of days. The chicks leave the nest anytime after they are twenty-eight days old. At this time they should be cracking seeds for themselves, but you should watch them closely to make sure they are being fed by the parent birds if they are not already self-feeding. As soon as you are certain that they are feeding themselves and are cracking seeds with no difficulty, they can be transferred to a flight cage for hardening up. There they will exercise their wing muscles and come into full plumage.

Budgie chicks should be banded as soon as the foot is large enough to retain the band. (For an explanation of how to prepare bands, see chapter 6.) Foot size varies with the amount of food the chick receives, and with the breed. Some of the very large imported Budgies may be banded when they are three or four days old. Others—most all others—could not hold the band in place until they are at least one week of age. You will have to use some judgment of your own as to when exactly to band the youngsters.

Budgies' toes are short, fat, and stubby, as are their lower leg bones. Sometimes you will have difficulty slipping the back toe through the band because the toe is so short. When this is the case, push the band as far up over the knee joint as possible, taking great care not to wedge the band too tightly on the knuckle, or to skin the joint. Now a sharpened pencil point may be inserted under the rear toe and with gentle pressure, pull it up through the band. The toe will bend like rubber, so you need not fear breaking it if you are careful.

With all the trouble it is to place the bands on the chicks, it is most exasperating to discover the next morning that the hen has removed every band and scattered them about the bottom of the cage. You can only repeat the process as many times as it takes for the hen to leave them in place. Avoidance of brightly colored bands will help, or dulling their surface with a non-toxic watercolor paint may help to conceal them long enough for the chick's foot to grow to the point where the hen cannot pull the band free.

There is not so much trouble in the case of Budgies, but often, in breeding Canaries, the hen will yank the chick right out of the nest in her attempt to remove the band, and, if you are not keeping a watch on the cage, the chick will chill or starve to death because the hen will not feed away from the nest.

Cockatiels breed much the same as Budgerigars, in that they will lay a clutch of eggs—provided they are in breeding condition—at any time of the year. They, too, lay their eggs every other day and begin to sit on them after the second or third egg is laid. The chicks hatch out as the eggs are laid, every other day.

Cockatiel nesting boxes are simply larger editions of Budgie boxes—the dimensions of a practical box being 10″ by 10″ by 14″ deep, with a 2½″ or 3″ hole for the birds to enter. The perch should be either ⅝″ in diameter or ¾″—the smaller size being perhaps better.

Both sexes sit on the eggs; usually the male sits during the daytime, and the female at night, with the male standing guard on the perch outside the entrance hole. If there is room inside the box, sometimes both birds remain inside at night, or even during the day.

Cockatiels come from Australia, and the ordinary, or "normal," bird, as it is called, is a very pretty gray bird, with white markings and a touch of yellow about the face in the female. The males have bright yellow faces with bright orange cheek patches when they are adult. Both birds have a crest, which, when erected, gives them a surprised look. The carriage and shape of the Cockatiel are most pleasing, and they make about as ideal a pet bird as one could wish for.

Cockatiels can be easily tamed if obtained when young, and they also will learn to talk. They live for a very long time. At the time of this writing the author knows of one male Cockatiel that has been the delight of its owner for twenty-three years.

One problem in breeding these desirable birds is that during mating the birds often fail to make contact in the act of copu-

Normal gray Cockatiels mating. This does not always mean you will have chicks. The hen shown here laid a total of thirty-nine infertile eggs!

lation. This is sometimes due to the thickness of the feathers around the vents. A simple remedy is to very carefully clip away all the feathers, especially the soft, clinging downy ones, from the vents of both birds. They do not like this indignity, but it does help increase the fertility of the eggs. I have one pair of Cockatiels who mate constantly, but the hen laid thirty-four infertile eggs before she and her mate were clipped. Some experienced breeders will tell you that, as a general rule of thumb, psittacine birds from Australia are usually easy to breed, while those from Africa are usually difficult to breed.

Now comes a group of birds from Africa to form the exception to this rule. These are the Lovebirds, of which there are many species. We will discuss the three most popular, and the easiest of the group to breed.

Lovebirds look like diminutive Parrots. They have the same general shape of body and beak and many of the same habits and characteristics of behavior. They will also learn to talk and can be tamed to the finger, but both instances require more time and patience with Lovebirds than with Budgerigars and Cockatiels. Lovebirds are usually hardy and live for a long time, and they are very colorful. Unfortunately, some of them are also very aggressive toward other birds, and for this reason must be kept to themselves. It is extremely difficult to sex Lovebirds, and even if you have two birds that make a nest and lay eggs, it is no insurance that you have a sexual pair, since two females will go through all the motions of mating and produce eggs in abundance—infertile, of course. Only if an egg hatches are you certain you have a real pair of breeding birds.

While Lovebirds will nest in a standard Budgie box, a good supply of nesting material must be provided, since they build elaborate nests within the box when the time comes. Strips of green bark, grasses, hay, feathers, squares of burlap, which the birds will strip into strands, are all accepted. Raffia, cut into 4" to 6" lengths is excellent nesting material, and this may be found in hobby stores throughout the country. Do not use just one type of material. They may not like it and will then fail to produce a good nest. If several kinds of material are made available, they will usually build the nest out of one of the stiffer varieties and then line it with a softer kind.

The best way to breed Lovebirds is in an outside aviary. If this is covered with heavy plastic sheeting on the top and three sides, they can be kept in such a cage the year round. In very cold weather, plastic should be hung over the fourth side as well. Use clear or white plastic rather than the black. Many of the Lovebirds are community breeders, but they will also breed as pairs in cages. They like a fairly large nesting box, or, even better, an old hollow log in which they can make their nest. Outdoor cages can be occupied right through the winter if the birds are placed in them in the spring and permitted to become acclimated as the seasons change. Protection must be provided from drafts and some sort of shelter given them during the winter, especially on freezing nights.

PEACH-FACE LOVEBIRDS are perhaps the most common species we discuss in this book and the most readily obtainable. They are also one of the largest of the group. They are pugnacious among themselves as well as with other birds and must be given room to dodge each other, so do not keep more than one pair in a fairly large cage. In an aviary, where there is plenty of flying room and where thickets of brush are provided as shelters and refuges, several pair may be kept together.

An odd habit these birds have is of tucking nesting material in among their tail feathers, then flying to the nesting box with them. The eggs hatch in about twenty days, and number up to eight in a clutch.

BLACK-MASKED LOVEBIRDS are second only to the Peach-faced species in popularity, and some breeders like the Black-masked ones better because of the more striking appearance of the birds. The neck, shoulders, and chest are bright yellow, and the remainder of the bird, bright green. The beak is a shiny bright red. The entire head is black and the eyes are surrounded with a stark-white ring. This contrast gives the bird the appearance of owlishly watching you all the time, and at the same time being slightly comical.

Black Masks breed easily in a Budgerigar box, although they do better in a hollow log. They, like most of the Lovebirds, build a rather elaborate nest out of twigs and grasses, filling the box to the point where they themselves have difficulty in entering.

Black-masked Lovebirds also differ from the Peach-faced species in that the former are very affectionate birds, both with themselves and with other species. They will mate and rear their young in large outdoor cages occupied by Cockatiels or different birds about the same size as themselves. The only time these creatures show any fierceness is during their mating time, and, if they are left alone by other birds, even at this trying season they go about their own business quietly.

There is a mutation of the Black-masked, called Blue-masked Lovebird. This one has a blue and white body, with the black mask and the white eye rings. The beak is whitish instead of bright red. They are not nearly as striking as the normal variety.

FISCHER'S LOVEBIRD is now the rarest of the three species discussed in this book. At one time it was very common, but for some reason or other the species died out to the point where it

Eggs of a Black-masked Lovebird beginning to hatch. Note the grass nest—unusual in psittacine birds.

A pair of Black-masked Lovebirds.

was very difficult to obtain a specimen. However, the birds breed so readily—nearly as easily as Budgies—that they are once more being found in pet stores throughout the country. But most of the breeding has been done in England and a couple of other foreign countries, and the supplies have been imported. With the new embargo on birds, it is possible that once more we will find a shortage of this delightful little creature here and have to depend on our own breeders multiplying the stock.

There is an all-yellow variety of Fischer's, mutated from the parent stock, which is also very beautiful. Fischer's Lovebird resembles the Peach-faced species to a large degree. The Fischer's has white eye rings, white cere, and a shiny red beak.

BEE BEE PARROT is also called the Orange-chinned Parakeet, and the Tovi Parakeet. It comes from Mexico and is a dwarf Parrot. They can be tamed, and some specimens will learn to talk rather well. They are an all-green bird with some blue and pale green on the body and a bright orange spot under the chin.

Bee Bees are community breeders and do not do very well in small cages. Perhaps two pairs would breed in a large flight cage, but I have never attempted to raise them this way.

These little birds are very curious and want to investigate everything around them, but, unless you have tamed specimens, it is very difficult to get close enough to handle them, and then you must watch out for a strong bite from their hooked bills. They can hurt.

Bee Bee Parrots are noisy little creatures but a lot of fun when you tame them.

One other difficulty—if it can be called that—with Bee Bees is the noise they make. When one tunes up, all the others chime in, and they have loud and raucous voices.

Records and Identification

6

If you keep a bird for a pet, there is no need to bother with keeping records, having a means of identification, sexing, or any other routine connected with it.

If you are breeding one pair of birds, the same thing holds. Since you have only one pair, you know which is the male and which is the female, and you know that the chicks obtained from them belong to those particular two birds.

However, if you intend to breed a number of birds for any reason whatever—that is to say, for your own amusement, or commercially—then you simply *must* keep accurate records of what you are doing, or you will become so fouled up at breeding time that your stock becomes hopeless.

I am referring, naturally, to the breeding of good stock, in individual cages. Not to the breeding in community aviaries for quantity. As I mentioned before, it seems pointless to breed poor-quality birds, since it takes exactly the same time and expense to breed a top-quality bird as it does a bum. Community breeding produces bums. Oh, there will be a fine singer once in a while, or a Budgie will turn up with all the good points, but these are rare exceptions rather than the rule. And even if you did get such a bird, how do you know which ones were his parents? How can you fix his strain?

Records can be as simple or as complicated as you care to make them, as long as you can easily interpret them. They may be kept in a notebook, a card file, or any other way that occurs to you, as long as they are accurate and kept up to date. They must be easily transferred to the cages at breeding time. You can use the method I described in the chapter on breeding Finches and Canaries. It is simple and easily maintained. Let me expand on my own method of cage records during breeding season, and you may use it or make amendments as they seem fit to you.

Using the peelable labels, I stick a blank one on the front base of a breeding cage. At the left end of this label, I write the band number of the hen placed in the cage, followed by a slant line, thus: 25/ . . . This label remains in place during the entire season. After the hen has been acclimated to the cage, and the partition put in place, the male is introduced on his side and his number added to the label after the slash line, like this: 25/18. I might mention here that my Canaries are all banded with odd-numbered bands on the females and even-numbered bands on the males, but they can be banded any way you like.

After the two numbers have been entered on the label, they remain there until the two birds have been mated and the laying finished. Now I begin with my color-coded labels as described in chapter 4. When the first egg is laid, a blue label is added to the cage, with the date the first egg was laid entered on the blank half. When the clutch is completed and the hen put to set, a yellow label is stuck on top of the blue one with the candling date on its blank half. The candling date being the seventh day after the hen is set.

When the eggs are candled, an addition is made to the identification label *if the eggs are fertile*. After the numbers 25/18, I put a circle, and within this circle the number 1, thus: 25/18 ①. Now I change the yellow label to the green one signifying that the hen is setting fertile eggs, the date the eggs are to hatch on the blank half, and the number of eggs she has under her written on the green half. The number 1 inside the circle means that this is that particular hen's *first* nest. When the eggs have all hatched, the red label bearing the date of hatching is placed over the green one. This red label now tells you that that particular cage has babies in the nest, so you can start your regular baby-feeding schedule. It is easier to go by a red marker on the cage, than to try to remember which nest has young in it, or having to look into each nest to find the baby birds.

If the eggs hatch on time and the chicks are reared successfully, the hen, in the normal course of events, will make her second nest in about 25 to 30 days. And, when this happens, the number 1 is erased and the number 2 placed within the circle. I do not take more than three nests from any hen during any season.

If all went well with the chicks, when they have been weaned and removed from the hatching cage, I enter in my ledger book that pair of birds by numbers, the number of chicks they had, the color given to them as a family marker, and, when they have been determined, the sexes of the chicks. These are the permanent breeding records. Later, I will add the disposition of the birds—as to whether they were sold, traded, shown, etc.

Before the chicks are removed from the parent birds, a colored plastic "family" band is placed on the leg opposite the one bearing the numbered band. The numbered bands are placed on the baby birds on the seventh or eighth day after hatching. These are bands bearing two identifying initials (these may be your own initials or those of your aviary name), the year date, and consecutive numbers. You may order the bands beginning with 01 and running consecutively thereafter, no matter how many years you breed, or get them beginning with 01 for each individual year. However you want your birds numbered is up to you.

Numbered bands are closed. That is to say, they must be slipped on the bird's leg while the foot is small enough to pass through the opening of the band. Only a closed band is a guarantee of breeding register, since it is known that a closed band *must* be put on the baby bird and cannot be changed after the foot has grown large.

Open bands are used for coding adult birds, birds purchased from other breeders, or special birds you are using for line breeding for color, form, song, or whatever.

Family bands are available in a number of different colors, with some companies offering two-colored bands. These are only available as open bands, and their main use is to identify families. When a hen and a male produce a nest of good, healthy, colorful chicks, a color is selected and a band of that color placed on the legs of each of the chicks, as well as on the hen and on the male. Then, when the birds are in their community flight cages, it is an easy matter to pick out the chicks from any parent birds, or the opposite—to pick out the parents of any particular chick. I always put my numbered bands on the right leg and the family band on the left leg, as a matter of habit—not that they *must* be put on in these positions.

Every so often you will find a hen that simply does not want to leave a band on her precious little chick. Every time you put it on, she will yank it off. This is frustrating, but there seems to be no way to stop the hen from doing so. You merely have to band the chick, then watch it closely for several days to make sure the band stays in place. Usually the next morning you will find the band on the floor of the cage, in the seed cup, in the nest, in the water cup, or tossed out of the cage completely, to roll around on the bird-room floor. The thing to watch out for is the chick.

If the foot was fairly well developed when first you banded the baby, the hen is more apt than not to yank the chick right out of the nest when she pulls the band off. If this happens, pick up the baby and warm it in your hands for several minutes. It must be good and warm before you return it to the nest. The hen will take it back with no difficulty, and, if it was not exposed to the cooler air of the bird room, no harm will be done.

If you are not watching for this to happen and the baby remains on the floor of the cage overnight, there is a good chance that it will die, either from chilling or from starvation. The hen will not feed the baby on the cage bottom.

I have had to replace the bands on some chicks as many as four times before the hen leaves them in position! And, yet, I have had breeders tell me that they have never had a hen remove a band from one of their baby birds.

Banding for consorts is done a little differently by me. Consorts are the chicks resulting from the mating of a crested bird with a normal bird. These chicks are then line-bred back to the mother and the father in order to obtain birds with crests. If you breed two crested birds together, the chicks will be baldheaded instead of crested. Instead, you mate a crested bird with a normal bird, then mate the daughters back to the father and the sons back to the mother. This is line breeding to fix a strain—in this case, the crest. Here I use two differently colored family bands, and use a personal system of placing them. For example, I am using a pale green and a dark blue band for my consort chicks during the year 1973. If the crested parent is a female, the green band goes on the numbered-band leg of the chick, on top of the numbered band. The blue band goes on the other leg. If the crested parent is the male, I reverse the position, placing the blue band over the numbered band and the green band on the other leg. The three bands on its legs do not seem to bother the chicks at all. Of course the plastic bands are to all intent weightless, and the numbered ones weigh very little more.

To get back to the cage-record system, if the eggs under the hen prove to be infertile, then the colored labels are removed, and the two birds are placed in separate flight cages for from four days to a week. The difference in time is determined by the condition the hen looks to be in. If she is not tired-looking, and seems fresh and perky, then four days is long enough to rest her.

Now she is returned to the breeding cage and the number of the male is erased. A different male is introduced and *his* number placed after the slash line on the label. The number within the circle remains 1, since it will still be that hen's first nest if she has fertile eggs this time with the new male.

If the eggs are infertile the second time, everything is repeated with a third male. If this third nest proves infertile as well, then the hen is retired as a breeder, being classified as a barren hen, and she may be disposed of at your convenience. This is, of course, if you are certain that the hen is old enough to breed, but not too old.

After the chicks are away from the parent birds and all the records entered in the permanent ledger, they may be put together in a large flight cage or singly in stock cages, as you wish, because the bands will identify them whenever necessary, and the record book will tell you all about the lineage.

The same system will work for any kind of bird you are breeding, only the bands will be different sizes to fit the different breeds of birds. If your desire is to rear quality Budgerigars, then by all means you should register with the American Budgerigar Society. Then you register your aviary and are given a code number. Now you will be able to purchase special ABS coded bands for your birds, and, no matter where they go in this country, the purchaser can always check the origin of the bird from the code on the band. This is a positive means of identification, and one that counts for a lot when exhibiting your birds, or selling them, whether as pets or as breeding stock.

Cards, printed especially for bird records, and in several sizes, are available commercially to save you the time and effort of making up your own. They have space for all the necessary information and make the job of record keeping much easier.

Incubating Eggs

7

Sometimes you may have eggs that you would like to hatch, but for some reason or other no hen is available to set them, or she refuses to set them. Often, too, breeders are given eggs by other breeders, perhaps of some rare species that a person has and is unwilling to part with, but is willing to let a few eggs go to another fancier.

These eggs can be placed in an incubator to hatch, and the chicks reared without the parent birds being present. With altricial chicks this is a great bother, since the babies, as soon as they are hatched, must be put on a hand-feeding schedule every two hours throughout the entire day and night for at least three weeks. They still must be hand-fed until they are weaned—from five to eight weeks, depending on the species—and the hand-feeding of baby birds is a real chore. Unless the bird is really a valuable specimen, it is hardly worth the time and effort to hand-rear it.

However, precocial chicks are a snap to hatch in the incubator. They are self-sufficient very shortly after hatching, and, while some attention must be given them in order to teach them to eat, this is only a matter of a day or so and then they are on their own. Indeed, some species of Quail and other small precocial birds fly within an hour or two after hatching! Button Quail are about the size of bumblebees the first day, and they can pass in and out of a normal cage as though there were no bars.

There are literally dozens of different makes of incubators on the market. Some of them are good; some are not. You should pay particular attention to the distribution of the heating elements in any you are thinking of purchasing, to make sure that when the tray is in one position it is not closer to the heater than when it is in another position.

Most incubators have some provision for turning the eggs, or at least, of changing the position of the eggs while they are maturing. Usually this operation is performed by tipping one end of the tray up, rotating the tray on an axle of some kind. Then, when the position of the eggs is changed, you merely tip the other end of the tray up. Eggs being incubated should have their position changed at least three or four times each day. More would be much better. When a hen sets her eggs, she is constantly rolling them around, turning them over and over. If an egg is incubated in one position throughout the entire period, the chick is apt to grow or stick to the side of the shell, making it unable to hatch when the time comes. The chick then dies before it can be liberated. Turning the eggs keeps the chick free inside the shell, eliminating this possibility.

Provision must be made to keep the air inside an incubator moist. This can be done very easily by placing a dish or two of water on the floor of the machine, replenishing the water as it evaporates. Some of the cheaper incubators merely have a bowl, a cover, and a screen trivet inside, upon which the eggs are placed, and water is poured into the bottom of the bowl. You have to open the incubator and turn the eggs individually by hand in this style incubator. From this model, they go on up in detail to the expensive commercial models which are completely automatic, with the eggs turned every hour or so by machine.

Whatever model you have, the thing to remember is that you must keep the temperature constant, the air humid, and maintain these two factors for the entire period of incubation. Eggs from different birds take different times to hatch—from twelve days for Finches to thirty days for a Peacock egg.

Incubators come in two styles—still air and circulating air. While I prefer the circulating-air type, many, many eggs are hatched in still-air machines. Kits are available for you to make incubators out of an insulated container. The kit supplies the heater element and a thermostat which, after the incubator has been assembled, must be set to keep the temperature at the proper level.

Different eggs should have slightly different temperatures, varying by a degree or two. But unless you are incubating eggs from extremely rare birds, keep the temperature from 101 to 103 degrees, and you should have no problem hatching nearly any kind of egg. The temperature should be read on a reliable thermometer, and it is important to mount the thermometer in a position where the stem is easily read by looking through the cover or window of the incubator, without having to open the lid. It is also important to have the thermometer mounted so that the bulb is at, or nearly at, the same level as the eggs, otherwise you will be getting an incorrect reading.

It does not matter if you have to open the incubator to service it, that is, replenish the water, turn the eggs, or whatever. Remember that a setting bird leaves its nest once in a while, to feed or to perform her natural functions, and the eggs are left uncovered for this time. The hen always returns to her job before the danger point of cooling occurs, and you must perform your servicing rapidly and close up the machine before the eggs cool more than a degree or two. Also, open the machine as little as possible, especially if it is a circulating-air type, since the fans will blow the hot air right out of the box, sucking in cold air which must be heated as it is blown over the eggs.

A day before the eggs are due to hatch, you must make some provision for confining the chicks to the hatching tray. Otherwise, if the eggs are from precocial birds, the chicks will scatter all over the inside of the machine, jumping into the fans and getting killed, drowning in the water dishes, and otherwise efficiently killing themselves in any way they can devise. A screened cover should be available to place over the hatching tray, and this may be put in place the day before hatching. Then when the eggs do hatch, the chicks should be left undisturbed inside the incubator for a few hours, four or five hours being long enough for them to find their legs and dry out completely.

A brooder must be ready to receive the chicks, and this must also be heated to a constant temperature. About the easiest way to make a brooder is to use a fish-aquarium reflector of the incandescent type, with bulb attached, suspended over one half of a cardboard carton. The other half is for space to permit the chicks to get out from under the heat if it rises too high and a place for you to put their food and water dishes. The temperature may be regulated by using differently sized bulbs in the reflector. You have a range of wattages to work with—bulbs of 100, 75, 60, 50, 40, 25, and 10 watts being available in any hardware store. You may experiment with the different sizes until you find the one that holds the desired temperature. Of course, you should do all this experimenting during the period the eggs are incubating, *not* after the chicks have hatched and need the brooder. You should observe the temperature over a period of several hours, at least, in order to make certain that the temperature is being held at the level you need.

The temperature should be maintained at 95 degrees for the first week, then lowered about 5 degrees each week thereafter until the chicks are self-sufficient, which is in about three to four weeks. After the chicks are dry and peeping in the incubator, they are placed in the brooder. Starter food and water can be placed in shallow jar lids. Tiny chicks, especially Quail, can drown in a quarter-inch of water, so provision must be made to protect them from this hazard. The easiest way to accomplish this is to fill the lid with a layer of pebbles or glass marbles. Then put the water in, and the chicks can dip their bills in between the marbles to drink, but cannot put their entire heads under the surface to drown. The bottom of the brooder should be covered with a pad of newspaper, torn to fit the carton, and a liberal supply of gravel sprinkled on the paper. The top two sheets should be removed every day and fresh gravel provided.

The chicks should be supplied with food at all times, and, although they do not have to be hand-fed, still they must be shown where the food is. This is done by tapping the edge of the food dish with a pencil point. The babies will come running over to look, and then you pick at the food with the pencil and the chicks will follow suit. You only need do this for a day or two, and the little creatures will then be able to feed themselves.

As soon as they can be removed from the brooder, you should put them into their runs outdoors. This, provided you are hatching precocials such as Quail, Pheasants, Peacocks, Partridges, and the like. Protection from wind and rain in the summer and from the cold, as in the winter, is important. After the birds are adult, they can shift for themselves all year in an outdoor pen, provided you give them some shelter from the freezing cold and wintry blasts of frigid air.

A list of incubation periods is given here, but remember that the time may vary a day or two, depending on the temperature at which you keep the incubator and the number of times you open it during the period.

Canaries	13 days
Finches	12 days
Budgerigars	18 days
Cockatiels	18–21 days
Quail	21–24 Days
Pheasants	21–24 Days
Parakeets	18–20 days
Parrots	25–30 days
Peacocks	28–32 days
Cockatoos	28 days
Macaws	28 days
Pigeons	16–18 days

Here is a list of bird-fanciers' societies in the United States—taken from a copy of the *American Cage-Bird Magazine*. The societies are listed by name, with the names and addresses of the secretaries.

INTERNATIONAL ASSOCIATIONS

International Border Fancy Canary Club. John F. Ross, 10091 Dixie Avenue, Detroit, Michigan 48239.

International Gloster Breeders Association. Mark E. Whiteaker, 516 East Seventh Street, Trenton, Missouri 64683.

National Institute of Red-Orange Canaries, and All Other Cage Birds. Mrs. Fran Titchie, 8820 South Wood Street, Chicago, Illinois 60620.

Toledo Bird Association Zebra Finch Club of America. Mrs. Phyllis Lexow, 4630 North May Street, Toledo, Ohio 43614.

NATIONAL ASSOCIATIONS

American Border Fancy Canary Club. Mrs. Madeline Mysliwiec, 1413 Britton Street, Wantagh, New York 11793.

American Budgerigar Society, Inc. Roy E. Oliver, 4424 Cane Run Road, Louisville, Kentucky 40216.

American Norwich Society. Frank Martin, 12114 Cantura, Studio City, California 91604.

American Singers Club, Inc. Mrs. Janet Commons, 410–31 Barrington Road, Wauconda, Illinois 60084.

Avicultural Advancement Council. Nona Naugle, Route 5, Box 5581, Bainbridge Island, Washington 98110.

Bird Association of California, Inc. Box 496, Bellflower, California 90706.

Central States Roller Canary Breeders Association. Marguerite Bowman, 1314 East Fifty-second Street, Chicago, Illinois 60615.

Cooperative Canary Breeders Association. Mrs. Jane Scott, 3659 Edenhurst Avenue, Los Angeles, California 90039.

Greater North American Color-Bred Judge Association. Gino Abbate, 136 Murray Street, Elizabeth, New Jersey 07202.

National Gloster Club. Mrs. Elmer W. Steele, 194 Wampatuck Street, Pembroke, Massachusetts 02359

United States Association of Roller Canary Culturists. Francis J. Kelly, 3729 Bronx Boulevard, Bronx, New York 10467.

Western Association of Canary Breeders. Mrs. Irene Evans, 13613 Ardis Avenue, Bellflower, California 90706

Yorkshire Canary Club of America. Mrs. William Mysliwiec, 1413 Britton Street, Wantagh, New York 11793.

Besides these national and international associations, the magazine lists clubs from twenty-four different states and Canada. These are:

ARIZONA

Cactus Bird Club. Eleanor Van Marter, 4161 West Hayward Avenue, Phoenix, Arizona 85021.

Kiva Canary Breeders Association. Frank McCaslin, 4531 North Fifteenth Avenue, Phoenix, Arizona 85015.

CALIFORNIA

Central California Cage Bird Club. Shirley Mahan, 1912 North East Street, Tracy, California 95376.

Combined Bird Club. Mrs. Marge Brinley, 124 North Allen, Pasadena, California 91106.

Fresno Canary and Finch Club. Eva Cobine, 22640 Elder Avenue, Riverdale, California 93656.

Nu-Color Bird Association. Charlene Massey, 11143½ Elliott Avenue, El Monte, California 91733.

Oakland International Roller Canary Club. Haig Sarkisian, 15148 Cooper Avenue, San Jose, California 95124.

Olympic Roller Canary Club. Charles L. Adams, 4932 Riverton Avenue, North Hollywood, California 91601.

Orange County Bird Breeders. Russ Sutton, 2091 Westminster Avenue, Costa Mesa, California 92627.

San Diego County Canary Club. Phyllis McClure, 359 East Madison Avenue, El Cajon, California 92020.

San Fernando Valley Bird Club. Mildred Erben, 901 South Mullen Avenue, Los Angeles, California 90019.

Santa Clara Valley Canary and Exotic Bird Club. Charlotte A. Le Doux, 665 Loma Verde, Palo Alto, California 94306.

Southern California Bird Club. Yvonne Saunders, 3523 South Centinela Avenue, Los Angeles, California 90066.

Valley of Paradise Bird Club. Mrs. Charlotte Joseph, 8505 San Vincente Avenue, Riverside, California 92504.

CANADA

Canadian Avicultural Society, Inc. Mr. E. Jones, 32 Dromore Crescent, Willowdale 450, Ontario, Canada.

Canadian Institute of Bird Breeders. K. H. Wagner, 15991 Perreault Street, Pierrefonds, Quebec, Canada.

Dominion Roller Canary Association, Inc. K. Swann, 9822 106th Street Edmonton 14, Alberta, Canada.

London and District Cage Bird Association. Miss B. Quick, 717 Maitland Street, London, Ontario, Canada.

Montreal Cage Bird Society. R. Kleber, 357 Govin Boulevard West, Montreal, Canada.

The Budgerigar and Foreign Bird Society of Canada. Mrs. B. Sanford, 17 Appian Drive, Willowdale M2J-2P7, Ontario, Canada.

COLORADO

Rocky Mountain Cage Bird Club, Inc. Rose Stults, 403 South Moline, Aurora, Colorado 80010.

CONNECTICUT

Budgie Club of Connecticut, Inc. Corienne P. Traver, 141 Hill Street Extension, Naugatuck, Connecticut 06770.

Western New England Cage Bird Society. Daniel Kaye, 29 Hamilton Drive, Manchester, Connecticut 06040.

FLORIDA

Florida Red Orange Canary Club of Miami. V. Perez, 744 S. W. Tenth Street, Miami, Florida 33130.

GEORGIA

Georgia Cage Bird Society. Mrs. Peggy Cochran, 706 Triple Creek Drive No. 7, Norcross, Georgia 30071.

HAWAII

Hawaii Bird Club. Box 3523, Honolulu Hawaii, 96811.

ILLINOIS

Greater Chicago Cage Bird Club. Mrs. Helen Symer, 5709 West Twenty-third Place, Cicero, Illinois 60650.

Illinois Budgerigar Society. Mrs. Beverly Leight, 420 Hoover Drive, Carpentersville, Illinois 60110.

Lou Abbott Roller Canary Club. Raymond A. Bowman, 1314 East Fifty-second Street, Chicago, Illinois 60615.

INDIANA

Indiana Bird Fanciers of Muncie. Mrs. Mabel Van Camp, 4389 North Olney Street, Indianapolis, Indiana 46205.

IOWA

Blackhawk Budgie Fanciers. Jack Simpson, 1724 East Thirty-first Street, Davenport, Iowa 52807.

Budgerigar Society of Iowa, Inc. Fonda Collins, Dallas Center, Iowa 50063.

MARYLAND

Baltimore Bird Fanciers. Mrs. Alvina Frey, Boxerhill Road, Route 1, Box 300, Cockeysville, Maryland 21030.

MASSACHUSETTS

John Wagner Roller Canary Club of New England. Mrs. Edwin Jones, 27 Highland Avenue, Arlington, Massachusetts 02174.

Massachusetts Cage Bird Association, Inc. Florence V. Steele, 194 Wampatuck Street, Pembroke, Massachusetts 02359.

MICHIGAN

Mid-Michigan Bird Club, Inc. G. Schneider, 1104 Herbert J Avenue, Jackson, Michigan 49202.

Mid-West Canary Club, Inc. Mrs. Marie Marra, 20567 Alcoy Street, Detroit, Michigan 48205.

Motor City Bird Breeders. Mrs. Ruth Ross, 10091 Dixie Avenue, Detroit, Michigan 48239.

MINNESOTA

Midwest Roller Canary Club. Mrs. Audrey Rauch, 1140 Raleigh Street, St. Paul, Minnesota 55103.

Minnesota Roller Canary Club. William H. Gronholz, Nicollet, Minnesota 56074.

MISSOURI

Missouri Cage Bird Association. Virginia Bowman, 3207 Franor, Alton, Illinois 62002.

NEW JERSEY

American Singer Club. Carl T. LaBella, 14 Pacific Boulevard, Cliffwood Beach, New Jersey 07735.

New Jersey Bird Breeders Association. Mrs. Mary Buntin, 179 Bevier Road, Piscataway, New Jersey 08854.

North Jersey Color Breeders Association. Helen Rombardo, 24 Prospect Street, Elizabeth, New Jersey 07201.

NEW YORK

American Singers Club, Chapter No. 1. Margaret Verdoleva, 732 Chester Road, Sayville, New York 11782.

Buffalo Canary and Budgerigar Club, Inc. Arthur Hodge, 281 Hamilton Boulevard, Kenmore, New York 14217.

Greater New York Roller Canary Club. Francis J. Kelly, 3728 Bronx Boulevard, Bronx, New York 10467.

Long Island Cage Bird Association, Inc. Madeline Mysliwiec, 1413 Britton Street, Wantagh, New York 11793.

New York State Budgerigar Society, Inc. Leslie Hamerling, 35 Colgate Lane, Woodbury, New York 11797.

Rochester Cage Bird Club. June Lang, 27 Valley Brook Drive, Fairport, New York 14450.

Trowbridge Cage Bird Society. Robert Chamberlain, 61 Palmer Road, Yonkers, New York 10701.

Buckeye Roller Canary Club. Sally Mills, 4476 Depot Road, Salem, Ohio 44460.

Columbus Canary and Parakeet Breeders Club, Inc. Mrs. Patricia Stinson, 201 Inah Road, Columbus, Ohio 43228.

Ohio Valley Canary and Budgerigar Club. Vella Mae Wisby, 3357 Merwin-10 Mile Road, New Richmond, Ohio 45157.

Toledo Aviculture Society, Inc. Sharon Riley, 245 Warrington Road, Toledo, Ohio 43612.

OREGON

Columbia Canary Club. Mrs. Clara Davis, 6543 North Greenwich Avenue, Portland, Oregon 07217.

PENNSYLVANIA

Delaware Valley Bird Club. Mrs. Jane Radcliff, 334 Laurel Avenue, Horsham, Pennsylvania 19044.

RHODE ISLAND

Rhode Island Canary and Cage Bird, Inc. Mrs. Helen Barbary, 78 Seven Mile River Drive, South Attleboro, Massachusetts 02703.

TEXAS

Texas Canary Club. Mrs. John F. Wisnewski, P. O. Box 625, Pearland, Texas 77581.

WASHINGTON

Avicultural Advancement Council. Nora Pringle, 20462 258th S. E., Maple Valley, Washington 98038.

Cascade Canary Breeders Association. William J. Skinner 4225 164th St. S. W., Alderwood Manor, Washington 98036.

WISCONSIN

Badger Canary Fanciers. Arno C. Tellier, Sr., 8200 West Congress Street, Milwaukee, Wisconsin 53218.

These are certainly not all the bird clubs in the United States, but they are the only ones listing themselves in *American Cage-Bird Magazine.* You will be able to find organizations in your area, or you might even start a club if no one is within convenient traveling distance of your home. A letter to one of the national clubs, or a letter to the editor of the magazine, should bring you any information you need on how to start a bird club. Interested persons around you who breed birds for a hobby or business can become prospective members, and you will be able to learn from them, too.

Birds are exhibited through clubs which hold annual shows, judged by accredited judges, either on a voluntary basis, or hired for a fee for the exhibit. Usually there are several classes in each show, from novice up through intermediate to champion. There is another class called open, in which birds you have purchased, but not bred, can be shown. Some shows do not permit this division.

Before you begin to show your birds in competition, you must find out the particular rules of the club and show you belong to. If your club is newly formed, then the members can ask for the showing rules from an established club and go by them.

Usually special show or exhibition cages are required, and these are either made to specifications or purchased. The birds, of course, must be in perfect condition, or it would be useless to show them. Remember that any bird entered in a show is competing with many other birds, some of them entered by experienced showmen and breeders.

Shows in other cities often will accept birds shipped to them for competition. Naturally, you are taking a chance when you ship your bird, but for the most part you may depend on your bird being given good care and attention when it arrives at the exhibit. Some exhibitors ship birds to several shows at the same time, trying for top honors in order to improve their breeding stock.

Often, too, a breeder will enter his birds in a show for the purpose of selling them after they take ribbons or honors. You may be able to pick up some very good breeding stock in this manner. You should by all means make an attempt to attend a show or two if only to look at the birds on display, taking note of the qualities that make winners. You can learn much about what makes up a good bird.

Crows will eat anything they can swallow. This fledgling was raised on canned dog food.

Some birds will become tamer than others, and most of the psittacines will actually become very affectionate and tame toward human beings to the point where they seem to prefer the company of their owners rather than that of other birds of their own species. It is fairly easy to tame a Budgerigar, Cockatiel, and some of the Parrots; and besides taming them, you can, with patience and perseverance, teach them to talk!

Finger-trained birds—those that will sit on your finger, or ride on your shoulder, whenever you wish—are much more expensive than ordinary birds of the same kind. If you are raising birds to sell, it might pay to put the extra time and effort into making them tame so you can get higher prices for them.

Some birds tame up if you hand-raise them. Crows, for example, when obtained as fledglings and hand-fed to maturity, will become so tame as to be almost a pest. You won't be able to move without the bird being underfoot. They make excellent watchdogs, raising a rumpus whenever anyone approaches the house. On the other hand, they make so much noise as to nearly drive you up the wall when you want peace and quiet. Crows can be taught to talk. Pay no attention to the old tale that to teach a Crow to talk you must split its tongue. This is not only not true, it is an unnecessary cruelty to the bird. A Crow can manage to talk perfectly well with a whole tongue.

Mynah birds are also able to talk. Teaching these birds and Crows requires much time and patience, but the result is a bird that finds it difficult to keep its mouth shut.

The secret of taming a bird is to get it when it is just out of the nest, feeding itself, before it has had time to pick up fear of humans from the adult birds. The parents of a bird you want to tame may be wild and completely unmanageable, but that will not stop the young bird from becoming perfectly tame and docile with a very little bit of attention.

To finger train a Budgie or a Cockatiel is simplicity itself, and the method is used for other birds as well. Other birds just take more time than do the little Budgerigars or the colorful Cockatiels.

As soon as the young are feeding themselves, the chicks you wish to finger train are put into individual cages. Now you have to make up your mind as to whether you are going to clip the wing feathers or not. This seems to be a matter of preference among breeders and trainers. Some say that clipping the wings makes the bird so insecure that one has difficulty in managing it during training. Others say that it makes the bird more easy to manage, since it soon learns it cannot fly and pays attention to the training as a consequence.

I would say that a lot depends on the bird itself. If it persistently tries to fly away while you are training it to sit on your finger, then, certainly, wing clipping is the answer. If the bird is naturally docile and tractable, then the clipping is unnecessary.

Just in case you do want to clip, however, the feathers that are cut away are the flight feathers of one wing only. These are the stiff primaries on the front of the wing, and the outer ends are cut off—not the entire feather. Each quill is hollow for a part of the length, but at the base it is filled with blood vessels. If you cut past this point, the bird will bleed pro-

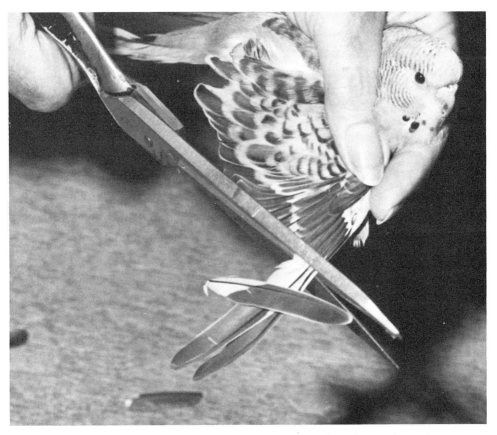

Clip the outer ends of the flight primaries of one wing only, to stop a bird from flying all the time, when you want to tame it.

fusely and suffer pain. It is as painless as clipping your finger-nails, to cut off the outer half of the feathers, however. Use a heavy shear because the quills are tough. If the bird is afraid, to restrain it you should wrap it in a towel, with one wing exposed, while you cut. This way it is more difficult for the bird to bite you, which it may try to do while being subjected to the indignity of clipping.

If you are yourself afraid of being bitten by a bird, then certainly you must either overcome this fear or let someone else train the bird because you will only be asking for trouble. Bear in mind that when climbing around a tree in the wild, or its cage in captivity, a psittacine bird uses its beak as a third hand or foot. It reaches out, takes hold of the new support with its beak, then pulls its body up to the position where it can take a new purchase with its feet. The bird is not trying to bite you, but the beak is hard and sharp, and the nip you get depends upon the weight of the bird. If he is heavy, he must grab hard to pull himself up. A light bird needs a lesser grip.

When you offer your finger to the bird, he grabs it with his beak, then yanks his feet up afterward. If you jerk your finger back as he attempts to take it in his beak, this frustrates the creature. No animal will tolerate teasing for very long, including yourself. After you have yanked your finger away enough times to arouse your pet, he will finally snap at it with a vengeance, and then you will really feel what it is like to be bitten by a hook-bill!

If it reaches for you, let it take hold. The grip will not hurt, or, at any rate, not hurt very much, and, as soon as he has a good grip with his feet, he will let go with his beak.

When you have clipped your bird, put it back into its separate cage for a couple of hours. Then the finger training can begin. Put your hand inside the cage with one finger extended in front of the bird. If he does not step up on the finger, nudge him just at the tops of his thighs, and, as you push gently backward, he will step up on the finger to keep his balance. Remove your hand slowly from the cage, with the bird on your finger.

You should keep up a steady conversation with the bird as you handle it, using simple words and a soft, even tone of voice. Since the hearing range of birds is more toward the high end, pitch your voice as high as you comfortably can when talking to it, or the sounds will be inaudible. It is for this reason that girls usually make better trainers than men. Their voices are pitched higher.

It is best to sit on the floor when first training a bird. That way it will not fall so far if it flies from your finger. Remember that it is a very young and very little creature, and until it has become used to using its wings, it can fall just like a human baby.

The lessons should occupy not less than one full hour, and it will be a good idea to place a clock where you can see it from the position on the floor. The reason for this is that ninety-nine people out of one hundred cannot accurately estimate elapsed time, and, after working with the bird for what seems like half the day, you will be shocked and surprised to find that only fifteen or twenty minutes have passed.

Work with the little bird until it sits on your finger facing you. Then use the other hand to extend a finger in front of him, and push against his body until he steps up on the second finger. Keep up your running talk as you work. Keep repeating the transfer from finger to finger. Some trainers advocate the use of a key word every time you make the bird step onto a finger, such as "Step," "Hop," "Up," or any simple word, to condition the bird to what he is supposed to do. The use of key words is fine except that there is the good possibility that the bird will not step onto anyone's finger after it is trained unless the same word is used each time. This means that the key word must accompany the bird throughout its entire life, passing from owner to owner. Without it, the bird may not respond to handling.

The first day should be enough to finger train a Budgerigar or a Cockatiel. Perhaps two or three days are needed for larger Parrots. The next step in training is to put the bird on your shoulder, spending an hour at this training, the same as with the finger. You simply keep repeating the process of placing it in position, talking to it all the time. Soon it will perch by itself, with no attempt to fly away, and then you may get up and slowly walk around the room, with him riding your shoulder. As soon as the training is over, the bird should be handled by as many other people as possible, using the same motions and words, so it will lose fear of all people, not just of its trainer.

In training a Parrot, you should use a short perch of wood instead of your finger. One reason for this is that the Parrot's beak is stronger and larger than the beaks of small birds like Budgerigars and therefore capable of giving you a more severe pinch. It may even draw a bit of blood, especially if the bird is startled while you are trying to train it.

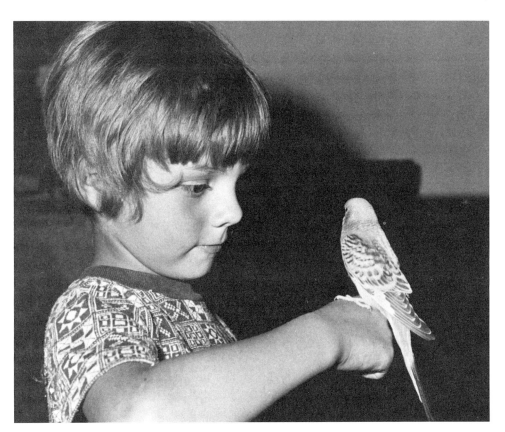

A tame Budgie makes a wonderful pet for children.

Anyhow, the perch eliminates this danger, and you will note that the Parrot takes a secure grip on the perch, then tries to move it before he steps on it. Birds like a secure perch and hesitate to step onto anything that may fall away from beneath them, so hold the perch securely in your hand while training your bird.

Food, especially one of the favorite foods of that particular bird, is always a big help in training. Offer a bit from your fingers as you work with the creature, when you want him to step forward to the perch, step on your finger, or your shoulder. If you see he is getting nervous, the food will help to calm him down considerably. Always offer the food from your fingers. I won't give you my opinion of people who feed their birds food from their own mouths. Let it be enough to say that if they are bitten on the lip or tongue, it is just what they are asking for. This is to say nothing of the mutual passage of diseases or germs if they happen to be present.

All the finger and shoulder training should be completed before you attempt to teach a bird to talk. They must first have overcome all their fear of humans and be docile and manageable. Talking takes a long time—as long as a year or even more in some cases.

The bird should be confined in a cage that is covered to exclude all outside influence. It must be kept in a room away from other birds, and where it cannot hear other birds' noises. A white cloth over the top and three sides of the cage should be enough. The front is left open for the regular maintenance chores, and to let you observe the bird.

Begin by repeating a simple word, or, at most, two simple words, such as "Hello, there," or, "Pretty bird," or anything else that you like. The words should be repeated many, many times, and every time you approach the cage. When you change the food and water keep repeating the words. Do not say anything to the bird except the words you are trying to teach it to memorize. Weeks, and sometimes even months, may pass without the bird saying anything except a squawk or two. Sooner or later, however, you will hear the little fellow softly repeating his new vocabulary. Continue to repeat the words to him until he says them clearly and frequently. Each time he talks, you might give him a bit of choice food as a reward. Perhaps a piece of whatever fruit he most likes.

One thing you must be made aware of, if this is your first attempt at teaching a bird to talk, is that the bird's voice does not sound like the voice of a human being. First of all, the bird's vocal apparatus is differently put together than yours, and next, the bird is quite considerably smaller than even a human baby. The voice of a Budgerigar, for example, is very tiny and thin, and it takes some practice for you to distinguish the words at first. Soon, however, you will clearly understand the creature when it talks.

The next important thing in training birds is to continue its vocabulary as soon as it has learned the first word. There seems to be a wide ability in Parrots and parrotlike birds to learn, once the ice is broken, and you can teach the bird whole sentences, questions and answers, poems, whatever strikes your fancy. Remember that the bird has absolutely no reasoning power, nor is it able to make up sentences of its own. It is a mimic, pure and simple, and will faithfully mimic what it has been taught, or what it has heard, but no more.

Perhaps the easiest way to start training is to obtain a training record, of which there are many on the market. Most of them are good, but you should avoid those which are not repetitive. These records have a simple phrase which is repeated over and over. Such a device placed on an automatic phonograph can run for as long as you can stand it. It is even better if you can go outside while the bird is having the phrase dinned into its memory. As soon as the bird has picked up that particular phrase, the record playing is stopped, and you then begin to talk to the bird, using the identical words from the record, and trying to use the same inflection of voice.

When the bird responds to your voice as it did to the record, then the second side of the record is put on and the process repeated. After the bird responds to the second lesson, you can either go on with advanced-training records, or go on by yourself. If you have the time and patience, it is better for you to take over the training after the bird has come to know what is expected of it. If you haven't, then by all means continue with recordings until you have exhausted the supply of them, and then you will have to improvise from that point. Records should be played to the bird for about an hour in the morning and for the same period of time in the evening before dusk.

Training without records should also be given in two sessions, as much to rest yourself as to rest the bird. One half hour in the morning and the same in the evening should be enough for both of you. During the training time, no one else should be around, of course, and if other people are in the house, you and the bird should go someplace where their voices cannot be heard. As you talk to the bird, you should hold him on your finger, facing you, and close to your face so he can watch your mouth to know that the sounds produced are voice sounds.

Since the first training you gave it was finger training, this should present no problem at all. And remember, as it learns more words, the learning progresses more and more rapidly. There seems to be no limit to the number of words and phrases a psittacine bird can learn.

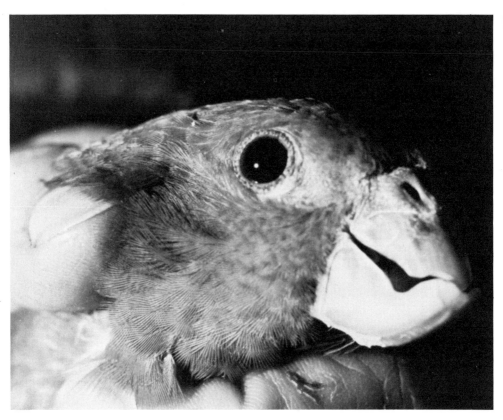

This poor sufferer has a deformed bill which must be trimmed constantly in order to permit it to crack its seeds.

Birds become ill just the same as human beings, and, while something may be done to help some conditions, it is far better to try to prevent illnesses than to try to cure them. As with all animals, in order to cure a disease you must first be sure just what the disease is, and this means you have to learn the symptoms and perform an accurate diagnosis. In some cases, taking a suffering bird to a veterinarian who is familiar with bird diseases will yield a diagnosis and treatment schedule, but usually the treatment is up to you alone.

If symptoms of illness are caught at an early stage, effecting a cure is far simpler than if you wait until the bird is far gone in its ailment. Your birds should be observed often. Healthy birds should have bright eyes, a perky, alert manner, be frisky, hop about their cages, and sing often if they are singers. A sick bird has dull or droopy eyes, ruffled feathers, or a puffed-up appearance, acts listless, sometimes with its head tucked under a wing, or sitting with its eyes closed most of the day.

As soon as any of these symptoms are noticed, you should take some first-aid measures. The most important of these is warmth. A bird's body temperature is high—102 degrees and higher—and, unless it is kept warm, it will lose interest in feeding. If this happens, the bird will fail rapidly, since the metabolic rate of birds is extremely high.

A healthy bird assimilates its food in a short time, which maintains its high body temperature automatically. A sick bird, however, eats less, and, as a consequence, lowers its metabolic rate to the point where external heat must be supplied in order to keep it alive. This may be in the form of a heating pad placed under the cage, a light bulb suspended inside the cage, or by any other practical means that may occur to you.

The bird should be isolated from your other birds by placing it in a "hospital" cage in another room, out of drafts and excessive activity. A section of old sheet, or an old towel, may be draped around three sides and the top of the cage to hold in any warmth provided. If you suspend a light bulb inside the cage, use one not over 25 watts in size, and take care that the bulb does not rest against any fabric cover used. There would be danger of the fabric igniting from the heat of the lamp. By far the safest and easiest to use is an electric heating pad. Taking the cloth cover off the pad will help, since the rubber base cover will be easier to keep clean. If the bird being treated is one of the psittacines, take care to place the heating pad in a position which makes it impossible for the bird to reach it with its beak and chew a hole through, shorting the pad, and possibly electrocuting the bird in the process.

Hospital cages are available, equipped with built-in heaters, thermostatically controlled. If you have valuable birds, it would pay to purchase such a cage, since the cost of the equipment would more than be covered by the value of one of the birds.

Only a few things are needed to prevent most disease onslaughts. Cleanliness is of prime importance in the cages and room. All seeds should be kept in covered containers so that feathers, droppings, and other airborne particles will not fall into them. The bottoms of the cages and especially the perches should be kept clean. Water should be drawn fresh each time

Wear gloves when administering any medicine to large psittacines. They can really bite when they are frightened.

it is put in the cups, and the seed and water cups themselves washed as often as necessary to keep them clean.

Newspapers, cut or torn to fit the bottom trays of the cages, should be kept in the trays in stacks of about ten or twelve sheets. Sprinkle a handful of clean bird gravel on the paper, then, when cleanup time arrives, which should be not less than every other day, the top two sheets of paper are discarded, the gravel shaken out of the tray, a new handful sprinkled in place, and the tray returned to the cage.

Two or three drops of wheat-germ oil (vitamin A) in the seed cup daily will be very beneficial to the bird's health. Cod-liver oil will do the same thing, but the trouble with this is that it goes rancid very quickly, and the rancid oil may do more harm than good. Peanut butter is an excellent food for birds, and most birds relish it. A small dab on the inside edge of the seed cup will soon be cleaned up, or, if it is too much work for you to wash the seed cup daily, then the peanut butter may be supplied in a treat cup.

As far as medicines are concerned, there are a few that you can give to your creatures. Probably the most valuable of all is the soluble chlortetracycline—also called aureomycin. This is sold by pet dealers without a prescription and is most useful in the treatment of many bird ailments. As a regular treatment, when obtaining new stock, it is a good practice to give the new arrivals this antibiotic as a preventative, in the proportion of two teaspoonfuls of powder to a pint of water. The solution is given in lieu of the regular drinking water for one week, after which the birds may be placed on their regular clear water for drinking.

New birds should be put in isolation cages for at least four weeks after bringing them home, before putting them into your bird room. During this time the preventative dosage of chlortetracycline can be given, and the birds watched for any symptoms of disease or illness.

Bacterial diseases are particularly dangerous in the bird room, since they are for the most part airborne and can spread through an entire flock of birds in rapid time. The treatment of such disorders is sketchy at best, and the bird, even if recovered, is never the same as before. There is also the chance that the sufferer will be a carrier of the disease even though it has recovered, or rather, did not die from the disease itself.

Some bird ailments and the treatments for them are described here, but the reader should bear in mind that the suggested treatment is by no means a sure thing. Rather, it is the best one can do, and you can only hope that it works. It might work for one bird and not for another. This is not to say that the treatment is always at fault. The diagnosis may be wrong.

COLDS. The symptoms of cold in a bird are very similar to those in a human being—runny nose, bleary eyes, listlessness, and sneezing. The bird sits with its feathers fluffed up and head drooping. About the only thing to do is to put it in a hospital cage and raise the temperature to around 85 degrees, covering three sides of the cage and the top. Administer chlortetracycline solution in place of drinking water, and continue this treatment for at least two weeks. Two teaspoonfuls to a pint of water for the antibiotic solution.

PNEUMONIA. While a cold is a virus disease and pneumonia is a bacterial infection, the latter is often the result of the bird catching a common cold and becoming so weakened that it catches the more dangerous pneumonia. The treatment is the same as for colds, but you might increase the strength of the antibiotic by 50 per cent, that is to say, three teaspoonfuls to a pint of water, and continue the treatment for three weeks.

RICKETS. The main cause of rickets is the lack of calcium in the diet. This can be brought about either by the chick being given a calcium-poor diet, or perhaps by chilling when very young. The chilling itself would not cause rickets, but it would slow the metabolism of the bird to the point where it could not assimilate its food properly, thus resulting in a lack of calcium. Not much can be done to cure this malady, since, by the time it is discovered, the bones have already lost their rigidity and the bird is more or less helpless. Sprawling flat in the nest is one telltale sign of rickets. The kindest thing to do is to put the bird out of its misery.

PLUGGED OIL GLAND. On the upper side of the base of the tail, birds have an oil gland. This is used in preening their feathers. The bird picks up oil from the gland with its bill, then rubs it through the feathers as it smooths and combs them out. Once in a while this gland becomes plugged for one reason or another, and the oil backs up until the gland becomes distended and swollen. The cure is to remove the plug with a toothpick, then gently apply pressure on the swelling until the oil oozes out.

ASTHMA. This is usually the aftereffect of a cold, and the treatment is long and tedious. The bird has difficulty in breathing. It wheezes and heaves with every inhalation. The cure often takes six months or longer and consists of keeping the bird warm—85 degrees at least—in a covered cage, and using an electric vaporizer with a bird inhalant daily.

A Canary chick suffering from rickets. The only thing to do is to put it out of its misery.

SOUR CROP. Usually caused by a mold. Keeping a supply of bird charcoal mixed with oystershell and grit in the cage at all times will do much to sweeten the crop and prevent this ailment. To cure it, one teaspoonful of baking soda in a quart of water, given in place of the regular drinking water, will end the trouble in a few days.

DIARRHEA AND CONSTIPATION. While these two ailments may seem directly opposite, the treatment is the same for both. A simple laxative. Either one teaspoonful of epsom salts in a quart of water, or two or three tablespoonfuls of mólasses in a quart of water, is given in place of the regular drinking water for two or three days. Repeat in five or six days if the birds are not cured.

EGG BINDING. If your bird is kept under clean conditions, with proper and sufficient diet, there should be no instance of egg binding. Once in a while, however, this malady will affect a laying hen and, unless prompt measures are taken, may result in her death. If you have a laying hen, she should lay one egg each day until her entire clutch of from three to six eggs is laid if she is a Canary or a Finch. A psittacine bird should lay an egg every other day, from three to eight eggs making the clutch. If she misses a day before the clutch is completed, hold her in your hand and examine her vent. If she is egg bound, you will see the bulge of the egg at the vent.

Keeping the bird warm at all times, put a few drops of warm mineral oil, or olive oil, inside the vent with an eyedropper. Try to apply the oil all around the lower part of the egg. The bird should pass the egg soon after the application of the oil. If she fails to do so, or continues to strain obviously in her attempt, a gentle pressure above the egg should help her expel it. After the bound egg has been passed, the hen will continue to lay her clutch as though nothing had happened, and she may not ever suffer egg binding again.

SCALY FACE AND SCALY LEG. Scaly leg is more common to Canaries and scaly face to the parrotlike birds, but both may contract both troubles at times. Scaly disease is caused by a tiny mite which infects the bird, causing inflammation on the legs and the bare parts of the face and causing the scales to stand erect. The legs and face have a rough appearance and often the scales peel off in patches. Bacitracin or neosporin ointment rubbed into the affected areas will help soften the rough scales and kill the mites. The treatment should be continued for three or four days, then again in a week. The preparation sold commercially under the name Scalex is made expressly for the treatment of this ailment and should be of use in eliminating the trouble. Use according to the directions on the bottle. Severe cases of scaly face on Budgies can be

Scaly face makes a bird look very bad, but with persistent treatment it can be cured.

The treatment for scaly leg is the same as for scaly face. Both are caused by a tiny mite.

painted two times a week with tincture of gentian violet. Your druggist can make up this solution for you. Apply it with a Q-tip.

BROKEN BONES. Sometimes a bird will break a wing or a leg. Sometimes you yourself will break a bird's wing or leg. If the break is a simple one, as in the case of a wing, nothing need be done except to place the bird in a cage from which all perches except one very close to the floor have been removed. Food and water dishes should be open and placed where the bird can have easy access to them. The break will heal by itself in about ten days. For a simple break on the leg, a splint can be fashioned out of a stiff feather, matchstick, or short piece of wire, taped snugly but not so tightly as to block

This little Budgie had a broken foot which was never set properly. It now must live with it in this position.

A broken wing may be bound close to the body until it heals, as
with this female Cardinal, hit by a car.

the flow of circulation to the leg. The taping must be secured
well because the bird will probably pick unceasingly at it.
Compound fractures where the bone penetrates the skin are
much more difficult to treat and should be left to a veterinary.

There are many other diseases peculiar to birds, but they are
not within the scope of this book. Only after much experience,
both with the handling of birds and their treatment, will you
be able to try to save some sufferers. The best way to keep
your birds healthy is through scrupulous cleanliness in the
bird room and cages and plenty of the proper diet and diet
supplements. They need fresh air, but no drafts, and a lot of
light. Sunlight is very beneficial if the bird is located in such
a manner as to be able to get into the shade when it needs to.
Direct sunlight with no cover or shade will kill a bird, much
the same as it will an animal confined in the full rays.

Of the over 8,600 species of birds in the world today, only about fifty or so are practical specimens for people to keep at home. Of course, zoos and large aviaries are capable of caring for many more species, but as pet cage birds, the number is limited to those which will thrive in captivity and live their normal life span, even breeding and rearing their young.

Some of the more popular species are described here. All of them will be found in one pet store or another or from a breeder or private aviary. Not all of them are always available, and some of them are very rare. The prices of birds depend entirely upon the supply and demand. Canaries and Budgerigars are the two most popular pet birds, and the prices of these are lower than for other species. Some of the Lovebirds, also, are very popular and are in great demand most of the time. Perhaps the psittacine birds—Parrots and parrotlike species—lead the field in numbers of species in captivity as pets. The second in popularity includes the Canary and the Finches.

The reason for the great popularity of Parrots lies in their ability to learn to talk and in the fact that they are trainable and tamable. A bird one can handle and play with is immensely more popular than one that flutters about in a cage, going into a fit of fright every time you go near.

A few of the Parrots are very difficult to breed in cages, but some of them are not. Some of them will breed all through the year if kept indoors.

SENEGAL PARROT (*Poicephalus senegalus*) Habitat, Africa. A small Parrot, second in favor only to the African Gray Parrot. A combination of gray, green, black, peach, and yellow, this

A Mustache Parrot, so called because of the black "mustache" under the beak.

A Blossom-headed Parakeet is very colorful. The female has a gray head instead of the plum-colored one on the male.

gaudy fellow is an excellent cage bird and will breed in captivity.

MUSTACHE PARROT (*Psittacula alexandri fasciata*) Habitat, India and Burma and is also found in China. This bird is named because of the black band running around the throat under the beak. It is thought to resemble an old-fashioned mustache. Does well in captivity and will mate and rear young. Very hardy and can stand cold weather.

BLOSSOM-HEADED PARAKEET (*Psittacula cyanocephala rosa*) Habitat, India, Pakistan, and Burma. This bird is also known

This Indian Ring-necked Parakeet has not been tamed and so must be handled with a glove to protect your fingers.

as the Plumhead Parakeet, and in adult males the entire head is a rich plum-purple color. The body is green and yellow, and the long narrow tail is deep blue and green. A very colorful bird, bred in captivity, but, in my experience, very nervous and skittish. They will, however, tame up and lose this fear if enough time is spent on them when they are young.

RING-NECK PARAKEET (*Psittacula krameri manillensis*) Habitat, India and Africa. This is a very common bird in India, and has been fairly low in price in this country. Now, with the prohibition against imported birds, the price is apt to jump. A very sleek, elegant bird, soft green, with a narrow black ring around the neck. The females lack this ring. Ringnecks breed readily in captivity and will rear two nests per year.

AFRICAN GRAY PARROT (*Psittacus erithacus*) Habitat, Africa. Most breeders and bird fanciers will say that this species of Parrot is the best one for talking and for taming. The African Gray seems to have the greatest capacity for mimicking the sound of the human voice. It is very long-lived. There are several records of an African Gray passing down through two and even three generations in the same family.

AMAZON PARROTS (Various species of *Amazona*) The Amazon Parrots are named, not because they come from the Amazon, but for their generic name. Several species are kept in captivity.

MEXICAN DOUBLE YELLOW HEAD (*Amazona ochrocephala oratrix*) This is a very hardy species and can stand cold weather outdoors if properly acclimated. It is nearly as popular as the African Gray, and some fanciers claim the Double Yellow Head to be superior talkers. However, the

Double Yellow Head is not as reliable a talker as the African Gray. It does, however, make an excellent pet and tames easily. It breeds well in aviaries or large cages.

GREEN-CHEEKED AMAZON (*Amazona viridigenalis*) Popularly called the Mexican Redhead, this is a small Parrot and a very noisy one. However, it tames so readily and becomes so affectionate that its personality overcomes the racket it can make. It is difficult to breed in captivity.

The group of psittacines called Conures all come from the New World. They are distinguished from other Parrots by their large heads and their heavy beaks. Some of the Conures are very large, but a number of them are about the size of Lovebirds. They greatly resemble the Macaws, but the latter birds have large bare patches surrounding the eyes, while the patches on Conures are considerably smaller.

PETZ' CONURE (*Aratinga canicularis eburnirostrum*) Habitat, Western Mexico, this bird, also known as the Half-moon Conure, is one of the most popular Conures in the United States. It makes a good pet when obtained young enough to tame, but, if not, there is nothing much you can do with the bird except cage it to keep it from tearing chunks out of your fingers.

NANDAY CONURE (*Nandayus nenday*) From South America, this bird is bright green and black, with touches of red and blue. It breeds well, tames readily, and is a poor talker. It has a voice most raucous and piercing, and if you have the bird on your shoulder when he decides to screech, your ears will ring for a long time afterward.

Mexican Double Yellow-headed Parrots are favorite talking birds. Some people think they are better talkers than the African Gray Parrot.

The Jenday Conure is very colorful, tames easily, and makes an excellent pet.

JENDAY CONURE (*Aratinga jandaya*) This is truly a beautiful bird, its head a bright gold, breast orange, back green, and tail blue, green, and yellow. It comes from Brazil and is one of the most popular of the Conures. The Jenday makes an excellent pet, tames easily, and will learn to talk. If you can get a pair that are compatible, they will breed and rear their young very well.

There are nine species of true Lovebirds and all come from Africa. Some of them are very rare and costly. Some of them are very common and low in price. Fortunately, in this country, these latter species are excellent breeders and are beautiful and, for the most part, affectionate. They must be taken for training when very young—as soon as they are weaned—or you will have little success.

Lovebirds should be kept separate from other birds because of their aggressive dispositions. They are hardy and long-lived and are good species for the beginner who wishes to learn how to breed parrotlike birds. In most of the species it is almost impossible to tell the sexes apart. About the only sure thing is "Them as lays eggs is females." Experienced and professional bird fanciers can sometimes sex birds by feeling the width of separation between the pelvic bones, but this is not for the amateur.

PEACH-FACED LOVEBIRD (*Agapornis roseicollis*) Also called Rosy-faced Lovebird. This is the largest and the most belligerent of the Lovebirds, but, because it breeds so freely and is so pretty to look at, it is one of the most popular species in America. They do not develop their peach coloring of the face until they are at least six months old. They will breed in an aviary containing several pairs.

BLACK-MASKED LOVEBIRD (*Agapornis personata*) This bird, and a mutation of it, the Blue-masked Lovebird, are rivals in popularity to the Peach-face. They also breed freely. It is a beautiful species, with a black head and brilliant red beak, white eye rings, yellow collar and chest, and green body and wings.

FISCHER'S LOVEBIRD (*Agapornis fischeri*) Also very popular, but does not breed as easily as the other two species mentioned. It resembles the Black-masked Lovebird except, in the Fischer, the head is bright orange-red.

The largest birds of the Parrot family are the Cockatoos and the Macaws. Also, some of the most expensive birds are in this group. One of the Macaw species, for example, sells for $1,000 and more each if it is available. These large birds require very large cages and do much better in big outdoor aviaries. However, after they have been tamed, they will live quite well in a roost cage in the house, where they can move about, be talked to, and visited with, and perhaps be freed for exercise about the room at times, returning to their perch at night and for feeding and watering.

LEADBEATER'S COCKATOO (*Kokatoe leadbeateri*) Perhaps the most strikingly beautiful of the Cockatoos is this species from Australia, where, indeed, all Cockatoos originate. The body is enamel white except for the breast which is rose, as are the neck and underwings. There is a large crest with a yellow band in the center and a rose band above and below with the tips white. When the Leadbeater's Cockatoo raises its crest, each thick feather stands individually, and the effect is like an Indian's full warbonnet.

Peach-faced Lovebirds are ideal birds for the beginner to try to breed.

SULPHUR CRESTED COCKATOO (*Kakatoe galerita galerita*) This is the commonest and the most popular of all the Cockatoos. A snow-white body with a sulphur-yellow crest, which the bird frequently erects when approached. These birds are very hardy and can be kept outdoors the entire year in any but the extremely frigid areas. They become exceptionally tame and affectionate.

Macaws come from Central and South America. While they are amazing in their coloration and become tame, making good pets, there are several things against their favor as birds for the average person. For one thing, their dispositions are unpredictable, and they can be quite vicious. This fact, coupled with the large, powerful beak, makes the Macaw somewhat undesirable to keep, especially around children, who are apt to make sudden noises and movements toward creatures. Macaws do not like to be startled and show it by attacking if possible.

Macaws have been reared in aviaries, and the adults will rear their young diligently, provided no interference by the owner is experienced. Despite the abundance of these gaudy birds, the price has always been high and shows no sign of ever lowering.

HYACINTHINE MACAW (*Anodorhynchus hyacinthinus*) Very hardy and very rare. Nearly three feet long, the entire bird is a rich hyacinth blue, overlaid with a lovely iridescence. The beak is black, as are the feet. The Hyacinthine Macaw is one of the most expensive birds available, and to obtain a breeding pair of these beautiful creatures requires an outlay of several thousands of dollars. The young ones sell for $1,000 or more if the owner is successful in breeding them.

Ruffles, a Sulphur-crested Cockatoo, is very tame and affectionate. He talks, too.

BLUE AND GOLD MACAW (*Ara ararauna*) The Blue and Gold and the Scarlet are the two most popular Macaws and the ones most often available in pet stores or from fanciers. Both are very intelligent birds, and both are good talkers.

SCARLET MACAW (*Ara macao*) As mentioned above, this bird is very popular. It is sometimes called the Red and Yellow Macaw, and the plumage is brilliant, deep scarlet and gold. This bird and the Blue and Gold species are the ones most often seen in bird shows, where they are capable of performing astounding acts. Several zoos and bird sanctuaries throughout the country schedule regular trained-Macaw performances for public entertainment.

While the emphasis in this book is on birds that can be kept as pets, trained to be handled, or taught to talk, still many species are kept by bird fanciers for their beauty or rarity alone. A well-run aviary is established with two ecosystems— one arboreal and the other terrestrial. This simply means that in each cage in the aviary, birds that live in the trees and fly about are kept with birds that live on the ground and do not, or at least, only rarely, fly.

In this manner many more species of birds can be cared for, without the necessity of individual cages. Often two or more species of flying birds can be kept together, and, beneath them on the ground, two or more species of lower-level birds can live in harmony. Naturally, you would have to select birds that are compatible. It would be senseless, for example, to put tiny Japanese Quail in with Pheasants on the ground, or Finches in with Macaws in the upper levels.

Max, a Scarlet Macaw, is nearly three feet long. He is quite tame. He sits on Vicky Frey's hand, hoping for a handout.

Quail not only make good lower-level aviary birds, they make good eating too.

BUTTON QUAIL (*Coturnix chinensis*) This is one of the best lower-level birds for aviaries. These interesting little birds breed freely and will hatch and rear chicks if provided with a thicket of brush or branches under which the female may hide her eggs and incubate them without being disturbed by the other inhabitants of the aviary.

KING QUAIL (*Coturnix japonica*) Larger than the tiny Button Quail, these birds are very easy to breed. As a matter of fact, it is difficult to stop them from mating and laying eggs all over the floor of the aviary. Shelter in the form of a brush heap should be provided as refuge for the chicks.

ROULROUL (*Rollulus roulroul*) Also known as the Crested Wood Partridge, this elegant bird comes from Malaya, Java, Sumatra, Borneo, and Thailand. The Roulroul is a round-

The way to a Roulroul's heart is with a handful of mealworms.

This is a Silver Pheasant. Pretty but not as gaudy as some of the other species.

bodied creature with dark green iridescent feathers on the back and blue-black underneath. There is a deep maroon crest on the male. They must have insect food in their diet, which can be easily supplied in the form of mealworms.

RING-NECKED PHEASANT (*Phasianus colchicus*) This, and several other species of Pheasant, are good lower-level birds for very large aviaries. They must have room, being very large birds, and, naturally, they should be put into cages only with other species of birds which are able to evade or defend

Peacocks are supposed to live for over 100 years.

themselves against the sometimes pugnacious Pheasants. The latter will rarely pursue a victim up into the roosts or tree branches in the aviary. Some of the more spectacular species of Pheasants are GOLDEN PHEASANT (*Chrysolophus pictus*), GREAT ARGUS PHEASANT (*Argusianus argus*), LADY AMHERST PHEASANT (*Chrysolophus amherstiae*), and REEVES PHEASANT (*Syrmaticus reevesi*). The Reeves Pheasant is an astonishing creature, with tail feathers five feet long and over!

COMMON PEACOCK (*Pavo cristatus*) The beautiful and showy Peacock should be familiar to almost everyone. One or two of the enormous and colorful tail feathers used to ornament the mantels of nearly every fine home during the last century. The "eye" in these feathers has been employed as an

Touracos are not common and are, therefore, highly prized aviary birds. Zoos are always happy to get them, too.

art design since antiquity. Peacocks can be permitted to roam the yard untethered, provided you live in an area free from predators, or have your property fenced in. The birds will not stray, but wander about picking insects and tender shoots of

Mynah birds are great thieves, as are Crows, Jackdaws, and Ravens. They make good talkers, though.

grass. The spread of the tail on the males during courtship is breathtaking. Peacocks may live for over 100 years!

TOURACO (*Touraco hartlaubi*) There are several species of Touraco known, and all of them are a challenge to aviary breeders. These are upper-level birds and have very elegant, glossy plumage with iridescent colors flashing over them. The birds also have a crest which gives them a regal appearance. They feed on the regular diet of soft-billed birds, and some of the species adapt well to aviary life.

GREATER HILL MYNAH (*Gracula religiosa*) Habitat, India. This is one of the most popular pet birds in the United States,

A Pigeon Squab being fed by its mother. Daddy waits his turn to feed the youngster.

because it will, when tame, talk readily and clearly, even excelling some of the Parrots in this feat. Unless the bird is taken when young, it will not become tame, however, and before you buy any Mynah, you should make sure it is able to be handled. They are omnivorous birds, eating anything they can swallow and even choking on chunks too large to swallow if you do not watch them. If a Mynah is around a person who smokes, great care must be taken to see that the wily bird does not suddenly snatch the lighted cigarette from his fingers and gulp it down before anything can be done. This results in the quick death of the bird. They relish canned dog food; Mynah pellets are their staple diet, and mealworms, or any other insects, are eagerly eaten. Mynahs are related to the Starlings. Extremely difficult to breed.

PIGEON (*Columba livia*) Pigeons are almost in a class by themselves as pet birds. They require coops outdoors, and a large cage, together with a shelter of sorts from the worst weather and cold. There are about 200 varieties of Pigeons, mutations from one species or other of the Dove. The most popular varieties are: Homers, Pouters, Kings, Fantails, and Tumblers. Pigeons are grain-fed birds and thrive on chicken scratch and Pigeon pellets, obtainable in feed stores. These birds lay two eggs, two days apart, and incubate them for about sixteen to eighteen days. The young are fed by regurgitation. There are many special organizations and clubs devoted to the hobby of Pigeon keeping.

Then there are a couple of unusual birds that sometimes become available to individuals, even though they are not cheap in price. They are wonderful specimens to keep in a large aviary or outdoor cage, but are not at all practical for indoor cages. These are the Hornbills and the Toucans.

GREAT HORNBILL (*Buceros bicornis*) This is an ungainly-looking creature, large, with dull black plumage, and white markings on the wings and underparts. The bill is large and looks as though a second bill was placed upside down on top of the regular one, giving the front of the bird an unusual appearance. Because of the size of this bird—nearly four feet long—zoos and public aviaries are the main keepers. Only if you have abundant room should you try to keep a Hornbill or a Toucan.

SULPHUR-BREASTED TOUCAN (*Ramphastos sulfuratus sulfuratus*) This improbable bird looks as though it not only should not be able to fly, but even sit on a perch without falling over face first. The bill is enormous, projecting out in front nearly as long as the entire body. Some beaks of certain Toucans

Hornbills are ungainly-looking creatures but are a highly prized bird among fanciers.

are gaudy in the extreme, brightly colored, and weirdly marked. Actually the beaks are very light, being spongy and porous, and the birds are excellent fliers, as well as being able to climb. When taken young, they can become very tame and make excellent pets. After they have matured, however, they are very wild and flighty, and it is nearly impossible to tame them. The diet consists of Mynah bird pellets with fruits, vegetables, and some raw meat. They have enormous appetites, and you must make sure they have enough to eat or they will languish. Several other species of Toucans are available from time to time.

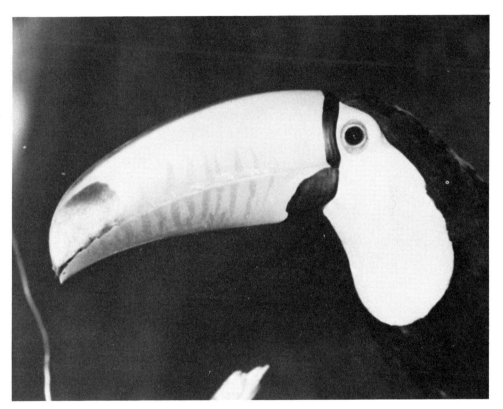

A Toucan's bill makes you wonder if the bird can ever get off the ground, but they are good fliers. The bill is very light and spongy.

WHITE-WINGED TRUMPETER (*Psophia leucoptera*) And last, but certainly not least, we discuss the wonderful Trumpeters. These are ground-level birds, living on the floor of the aviary. They become so tame as to make pests of themselves, running after you all the time, getting underfoot until you trip over them every time you turn around. They always want to be petted on the neck and head, and, when you settle down to really giving them some begged-for attention, they hum in contentment as you stroke their necks.

Trumpeters are long-legged birds, with bodies about the size

Trumpeters become so tame they do not have to be caged. They will stay around the house like a watchdog.

of the domestic chicken. They have large beaks but do not attempt to strike you with them. They are dull blackish-brown in color and are not really pretty birds. Their value and interest lie in their extremely affectionate manner and their endearing attempt to gain attention and coddling.

There are, of course, many more species that you will find one time or another on the market, or for sale at aviaries throughout the country. Once you have been introduced to the wonderful world of birds, you will probably be on the lookout for oddities and unusual specimens. Birds have fascinated mankind since before historical times, and still there is a lot to learn from these fragile winged creatures. And the reward of having a trusting little baby bird sit on your finger, fearless and contented, will far outweigh the time and effort it took to get him to that point.

PAUL VILLIARD, author of *Birds as Pets,* was born in Spokane, Washington, and now lives in Saugerties, New York. Although he started out as a mechanical engineer, he soon found that his real talent lay in writing and photography.

He has traveled for many years in the Pacific Islands, South America, and throughout the United States. From these years of traveling, observing, and photographing came much of the material for many of his books.

Mr. Villiard's beautiful photography and fine writing have appeared in *Natural History, Audubon Magazine, Popular Home Craft, Home Crafts and Hobbies, Reader's Digest,* and *Nature and Science* magazine, among others. His other books include *Wild Mammals as Pets, Reptiles as Pets, Insects as Pets,* and *Exotic Fish as Pets.*

A true renaissance man and writer, Paul Villiard's works cover the areas of crafts, manual arts, ecology, photography, and cooking, as well as other fields. He has written over twenty-four books in the past seven years and has had his work translated into Danish for publication abroad.

Index

Abbott, Lou, Roller Canary Club, 112
African Fire Finch, 70
African Gray Parrot, 147
African Whydahs, 72
Altricial birds, 5
Amazon Parrots, 147
American Border Fancy Canary Club, 107
American Budgerigar Society, 99, 107
American Cage-Bird Magazine, 107, 116
American Norwich Society, 107
American Singers Club, Inc., 108, 114
Anise seed, 32
Asthma, 136
Aureomycin, 134
Australian Fire Finch, 69
Avicultural Advancement Council, 108, 116

Badger Canary Fanciers, 116
Baltimore Bird Fanciers, 112
Banding, identification, 94–97
  of chicks, 82–83
  family, 96
Baths, bird, 15, 22
Beaks, bird, 10
Bee Bee Parrot, 91, 92
Bird Association of California, Inc., 108
Birdbaths, 15, 22
Bird-fancier's societies, 107
Birds
  altricial, 5
  beaks of, 10
  body of
    construction of, 7
    temperature of, 131
  bones of, 9
  breeding of
    bringing into condition for, 39
    in cages, 12

insuring compatibility for, 44
seasons of, for cage birds, 39
as carriers of disease, 2
with chicks, feeding schedule for, 51–52
descended from reptiles, 5–6
developing new strains of, 12
diets of, 6, 61, 62, 70, 71, 73, 75
diseases of, 131ff.
eating habits of, 14
embargoes on import and export of, 68, 91
exercise room for, 18
exhibits of, 116
families of, 6
feet of, 10–11
hook-billed, 6
incubation periods for hatching, 106
insectivorous, 30
orders of, 6
parasitic, 72
passerine, intelligence of, 6, 7
perching, 6, 11
  clipping claws of, 28–29
precocial, 5
prices of, 143
record-keeping for, 93
seedeater, 30
showing of, competition, 117
sick, treating, 132ff.
soft-billed, 70
species of, 143
sunstroke in, 20
susceptibility of, to drafts, 20
training, 28, 119ff.
  to talk, 126
  use of food in, 126
  use of recordings in, 127–28
vision of, 9
as youngest group of animals, 6
Blackhawk Budgie Fanciers, 112
Black-masked Lovebirds, 88, 152
Blossom-headed Parakeet, 145